THINKING PHYSICS THIS WAY

THINKING PHYSICS THIS WAY

WELCOME TO THE WORLD OF PHYSICS

KAPUR MAL JAIN

ISBN:	Softcover	978-1-4828-4280-7
	eBook	978-1-4828-4279-1

To order additional copies of this book, contact
Partridge India
000 800 10062 62
orders.india@partridgepublishing.com

www.partridgepublishing.com/india

Contents

Foreword 7
Preface 11

PART I: Nature, curiosities and birth of physics
1. Look around: curiosities get ignited 19
2. The World of Physics 24

PART II: Physics beginning to build, World beginning to change
3. Evolution and Transition 33

PART III: New insight! New vision
4. Magic Years! New insights! 63
5. Universe - new vision! 147

PART IV: Vicissitudinal Vistas
6. New roads: New Challenges 161

PART V: Inspirations and messages
7. Inspirations 171
8. Physics and Education: Messages 197
9. Motivational quotes and tips 221

References 229

Foreword

I felt much privileged when my friend Dr. Kapur Mal Jain wanted me to write foreword for his book 'Thinking Physics This Way'. Reading this book is indeed a unique experience. It holds in its pages last 300 years development in the field of physics. Dr. Jain starts his story of development of physics right since the time when primitive man saw activities of Nature with interest and curiosity. His curiosity begot queries about what was happening around. It is this enquiring mind of the man which has brought us step by step to the present stage of development.

The book encompasses developments in almost all the major areas of physics. Diverse ideas which gave birth to theories for explaining new phenomena or improving upon the old theories are so well put together that continuity of the entire book is beautifully retained. From Newton's mechanics through relativity and quantum mechanics, the author takes us to the regime of Quantum Field Theory (QFT) which is necessary when the system is quantum and velocities are relativistic. The developments in the field of Elementary Particle Physics are put together chronologically and logically for a clear and exact understanding of the subject. Ideas of unification of fundamental forces and theory of everything (TOE) also find place in the book.

Physics of Standard Model and Beyond Standard Model has also been touched upon in a very lucid manner.

Stories of conservation laws and field theories are also narrated in author's own interesting style. All the major advances in understanding diverse phenomena are included in the book. Along with developments in atomic, molecular, nuclear and sub-nuclear physics, elegant description of developments in the fields of cosmology and biophotonics gives completeness to the book. The latest ideas of dark matter and dark energy also find place in the book. The beauty of the book is that author not invoked upon any mathematical equation, graphs and formulae. Still the simple and straight forward descriptions by the author leave no room for confusion. Dr. Jain takes you very comfortably from Newton's Gravitation to the discovery of Higg's boson.

Author mentions about subjective experiences of Yogis and success of Homeopathy which are yet to be thoroughly examined and understood. The concluding pages of this book envisage about the role physics may play in augmenting the quality of life on the planet. Events from life of great physicists are chosen and included in the book to inspire students in their pursuits in the field of research. Physicists have unfolded many mysteries of this physical world still many more are yet to be solved every time when we know something, lot many things are left to be known. Such is the path of science. There is no destination in the path of knowledge. You reach one destination and come to know of newer ones to reach. Infinite are the secrets of Nature and one can unfold very little in his lifetime. The greatest of physicists Newton rightly said 'What I know is a drop and what I do not know is an ocean'. Reader realizes this fact while going through pages of this book.

Dr. Jain's book 'Thinking Physics This Way' will not only be liked by physics community but it would also be most welcome by the layman who wants to satisfy his curiosity about the developments in physics. I congratulate Professor Jain for this wonderful book and thank him for giving me privilege to write foreword for this book.

With Best Wishes,

Dr. Gopal Krishna Upadhyaya
Professor of Physics,
Vikram University, Ujjain (M.P.)

Preface

The observations of natural events and evolution of new ideas make the stand of Science. This 'stand' builds the world view of the universe. But it never remains rigid and changes with new insights and understanding. With each shift of scientific paradigm, it changes. From the history, we learn that the first scientific world view started evolving up from Aristotle's work. It prevailed for about two thousand years and then changed substantially after sixteenth century. The new-world view emerged in the twentieth century from 'bizarre ideas' and concepts developed during the study of micro-world.

In order to understand the growth of science, a logical flow is required. Scientists followed this flow and tried to explain the natural events and associated observations. Gradually the basic structure of physics has started emerging around matter and energy. They exhibit different characteristics, interact with each other in space and are engaged in retaining or changing their forms in time. Physicists make a systematic study of the events and discover the laws that govern the Nature and its working.

An event may be thought to have multiple connections with and varying influences by its surrounding. In order to understand, let us take an example of falling bodies. On the basis of our experiences, we can predict the path of a falling 'stone' but not of a falling 'feather'. Actually, the flow of wind and changes in temperature and pressure that are neglected while describing the motion of a heavier body (such as a stone) cannot be neglected while describing the motion of a lighter body (such as a feather). Thus, the understanding of any event requires knowledge of the relationships that connect the event with environment and the strength lying therein. Physics explores these relationships by taking the help from mathematics. If need be, physics creates new mathematics to get new insight. Physicists develop theories and then look for the 'exceptions' as they provide clues to understand Nature at deeper level. That's why physics undergoes a test with every new observation. Physicists welcome failures in their efforts because whenever they fail, they find nature disclosing one of its secrets. With each new secret, a new way of thinking and observing the nature emerges. Physicists start revisiting the age-old concepts in the new light. As a result, 'world view' always changes.

The very idea and exploration of physicists can never be rigid. It depends on the details of 'observations' and 'logic'. The logic, working at one point of time may not always stand. New logic and relationships are explored in order to understand every new phenomenon. So, there is no 'full stop' in physics and as a matter of fact it is always evolving and with pleasant surprises.

The last decade of the nineteenth century witnessed a major turning point that transformed physics. The physical laws developed to deal macro-scale were found untenable at micro-scale. So a new conceptual framework was built over next four decades. Soon, physics became the most influential subject of study. Today, none of the fronts; be it human, social or economic can be imagined without physics. The kind of world and technology that we live today could scarcely have been imagined by mankind and even visionaries a century ago.

The study of physics provides inroads practically in all disciplines of sciences like chemistry, biology etc. and is continuously providing us the 'resource points' that may be tapped. Some of them have wishfully been exploited by technologists in order to create a technological world around us. The tremendous growth in the areas like energy, communication, transportation, industry, environment, medicine, meteorology, defense etc. that we see today would have not been possible without physics. With this point of view, physics may be called as a 'technology booster' that we come across in a relationship between 'science and technology'. But interestingly, we also come across some 'life-building resource points'. They may be used to explore a new relationship between 'science and education'.

The very idea of this book is to fascinate and extend an invitation to all those who have penchant but scared of physics. Some motivational stimulation and sources of inspiration have been provided for them. This book introduces the readers to the inherent beauty and myriad magic of the subject and also provides them the way physics is created and conceived with an easy hands on access and can be made accessible. The readers will explore an innovative and fascinating journey to reach the frontiers of physics. Further, the readers will find a new relationship between 'physics and education', which may fill them with value-consciousness.

I dedicate this book to all my students, who have been an integral part of my every innovation and exciting journey of 35 years of teaching and academic career. I thank my friends Dr. R. K. Shrivastava, Dr. S. P. Bhatnagar, Dr. Mridul Bose and Dr. Anuj Hundet who have been the catalysts while writing of this book. I express my heartfelt gratitude to Dr. Anand Kumar Singh who gave me many valuable comments after seeing the preliminary version of the manuscript. He raised queries that I had not explained properly and gave many suggestions for improving the flow. He soulfully interacted very critically and gave inputs to sharpen the text making the presentation focused. The discussions on different issues with the participants in various refresher and orientation courses have also helped me in polishing and fine-tuning the material for the book. The discussions on the topic 'physics and education' with my friend Dr. Sanjay Tignath were most precious. I express my deep sense of gratitude for his suggestions and candid comments on this new relationship. I thank Dr. Meenakshi Choubey for proof reading and enriching the presentation. Thanks are also due to my friend Prof. G. K. Upadhyay who very kindly agreed to peruse the manuscript and to write 'foreword' for the book. The excitement and enthusiasm of my son Harshel, a student of MNIT, Jaipur has helped me understand the world of physics at deeper level. The contribution of my wife Aruna deserves a special mention because of her keen interest and inquisitive attitude towards the natural science, physics, from the general and layman's perspective. I am indebted to my teachers late Dr. T.N. Misra of Indian Association for Cultivation of Science, Jadavpur, late Dr. Y.S. Satya of IIT,

Delhi and late Prof. S. Guha of Ravi Shankar University Raipur (Chhattisgarh) who took me to the exciting world of Physics and remain guiding force all through my life. Last but not the least, I acknowledge and appreciate the valuable support of Partridge Publishing Company that facilitated the publication of this book.

Kapur Mal Jain

PART -I

NATURE, CURIOSITIES AND BIRTH OF PHYSICS

1

LOOK AROUND: CURIOSITIES GET IGNITED

Nature is full of pied beauty, sounds and fragrance and its exuberance is seen everywhere. When we move around, we feel attracted to the symmetry and beauty present in the Nature. The periodic and frequent advent of natural events allures us. The florescent colors, shades and patterns in butterflies, birds and flowers, patterns in dancing peacocks, fast changing shades of clouds in the sky, view of rainbow, variegated tints during ripening of fruits and vegetables call our attention. Warble of birds and voices of animals, the hue of rising and setting sun, changes during waning and waxing moon, solar and lunar eclipses, the tides -its ebb and flow make us curious.

Today we have satisfactory answers to most of these natural enigmas. But it was difficult for the human being in ancient times to find explanations of these natural events. Now, we can imagine the way mankind followed to understand these weird situations and experience the natural occurrences in day to day life through the help of Science and History. Primitive man had no tools except natural sensors like eyes, ears etc. There existed no technology other than 'natural tools' like teeth, hands, palms, fingers and nails to help him. He distinguished himself from animals as he possessed mental ability to think and discover. The ability to think and communicate his feelings in language imparted confidence to intervene and create. This intelligence played major role in developing his life qualitatively. He came out of shelter rocks and caves to huts and houses; though he hunted for food but started gathering surplus amount of food for the future. He used sharp stones or objects as weapons to protect himself from wild animals. A rolling stone's observation might have given the idea of inventing 'wheel'. Probably the 'jungle fire' gave the idea of generating fire from friction by rubbing wood or stone. Thus, the primitive man gradually traversed a very long distance from Paleolithic to Chalcolithic period and developed into a social animal. He formed tribes, created shelters, became farmer and partook in the process of human evolution. His continuously growing experiences made him believe that he had enormous prowess and potential to reveal the secrets of nature. The laws of nature remained secret till it was further explored in due course of time. This involved a greater amount of wisdom, intelligence and understanding of Nature around --the Nature that abounds on symmetries, patterns, physical forces and visible changes. The hidden behavior of Nature aroused some original questions and compelled to find real answers. This 'process' is the process of science.

Let us take the example of symmetry found all around in Nature. We feel attracted to the symmetry that exists everywhere in Nature. Our own body is a good example of symmetry. Spider-web, flowers, honeycomb, snowflakes etc. are the examples of symmetrical patterns. Actually, we inherently love symmetry as it gives us peace and good feelings. This is the reason why we hanker to find symmetry in everything. We unknowingly put our efforts in bringing the symmetry. If we look in the recent past, we find that symmetry gave many scientific ideas and thoughts. Even in today's scientific world, symmetry works as a guiding and driving force. Almost this was the mental state of ancient man when he found symmetrical 'patterns' and 'periodicity' in Nature by close and careful observations.

Symmetrical patterns emerge from internal 'arrangements'. Further the arrangement changes the patterns and affects our feelings. By merely changing the position of articles in a room we notice change in perception. New properties, beauties, symmetries and even way of life appear altogether modified by simple alterations in patterns, habits and routine. Therefore, meaning behind the 'arrangements' is of paramount importance to understand the inherent suggestions. We can think of consequences of changing the 'order' of the ingredients in the arrangements. To understand it better, let us take an example of torch. On reversing the polarity of the battery used, torch doesn't give light. So, we realize the importance of proper 'order' and their arrangement. Since the very beginning man understood this orderliness and hidden connections in Nature. He remained watchful and continued taking finer observations of the happenings around him.

Understanding Nature from its very beginning got prominence. To put in modern terms, natural phenomena pervaded like mega e-library where every physical part i.e. mountains, oceans, rivers, trees and their seed, stone, or sand, behaved like 'folders' containing numerous 'sub-folders' and infinite number of 'files' which remained inaccessible due to the 'coded language'. We can assume of hard diligence that was put forth to decode these files of Nature. Owing to varied taste and aptitude these files were decoded further which ensued a voluminous range of natural clues not only in the form of motion, light, sound, and colors but also in many other mysterious forms or laws of nature.

Gradually, the man started getting answers to a number of questions: Why do things fall? Where do the clouds come from? Why is there thunder and lightning in the sky during rainy or stormy days? How the rainbow is formed? Why is there fog in morning's atmosphere during winter? Why do we feel heat when palms are rubbed together? Why does the colourful world become colourless during new moon's nights? Why does water exist in different forms but air in only one form? Every answer entailed new array of queries for further enquiry with no feeling of complacency at all. In order to find not only the answers but the real cause behind the events, a logical path was developed and followed. This led to proper understanding of cause and effect that further helped in predicting new phenomena. The predictions set to test the theories and their validity. And, a process for designing and conducting the experiments skillfully under controlled conditions was evolved.

While developing suitable theories, relationships between different observations led to explore new type of relationships that emerged out in the process. Some of them were of technological importance. For example, a correlation of wood plank to float in the water and the blowing wind accrued to emergence of 'water transport' facility. We have seen many such relationships being explored and used advantageously. Thus, with the passage of time, a body of scientific knowledge started taking shape. And, with increasing understanding of Nature and its underlying processes, a parallel world of choice and fancy is created. Today we apparently observe both worlds side by side. We see and feel the natural and man-made worlds compatible in our surrounding with this fusion and continuous evolution. As a result, now a new age of human civilization had dawned on our planet Earth.

2

THE WORLD OF PHYSICS

Mankind's curiosity knows no bounds and is inexhaustible. The desire to know the functions of Nature begot many questions. Consequently 'What?', 'What not?', 'Why?', 'Why not?' and 'How?' got prominence. But finding the logical answers to such questions is not so easy. Nature's physical manifestation is elegant and organic, intrinsic and holistic as it expresses its widespread interconnectedness in very simple forms; but for proper analysis, it was reduced into systems of 'machine' which was assumed to be made of separate parts connected weakly with one other. It was expected that understanding the 'parts' fully might lead to understanding the 'whole' system. This view is called 'reductionist view' in modern terms. This view worked initially to fetch answers in response to interrogations of why and how. This approach culminated into forming logic to understanding Nature and its laws in depth. These collective efforts gave birth to 'physics' as discipline. Though physics is fascinating, but to grow into a 'physicist' one requires a lot of patience and careful analytical power.

The Physicists

Physicists are given to perform like detectives. Like them, they exert to espouse their observations foolproof so that their experiments, analysis and correlations are methodically correct. After this, they discover the links between the various observations and hypothesize the missing links, if necessary, to propound the theory. They propose theory in clear and logical manner and give thorough interpretations. They predict the outcome in the form of experimentally verifiable conclusions.

The symmetries provide initial clues and guidance to physicists. That's why they excavate symmetry to develop theories and make predictions. In recent past many instances we see that helped physicists in making predictions from symmetry based ideas and logics.

Physicists carefully observe and analyze the clues like 'forensic scientists' who develop right interpretations logically by taking the tiniest clue into account. Their ultimate objective is to find out the truth lying in the incidents that took place. The physicists also do the same. They use clues from the available information to proceed logically and discover unknown facts. Today, we know much about 'shining stars' in the sky which are beyond our reach. We only receive twinkling light from them. But, this becomes a clue for Physicists. Through their analysis of light, we now know that all stars are made of the same material. They take birth, live a life and expire. The same clue 'light' could lead us to know about the birth of the universe and its expansion since then.

If we trace back the history, we find that the basic knowledge about the working of Nature was attained when technology was not much developed. After acquiring knowledge, physicists made apparently complicated phenomena and processes simple and comprehensible. Physicists were able to predict logically the conditions for a particular event or effect to occur. The researchers and experimentalists confirmed and established that the structure of physics is actually nothing but the web of fantastic and fascinating logics.

The logic of physics

Physics is the wonderful exploration of youthful and innovative mind irrespective of age and gender. Physics flourishes in free environment. The more one knows the facts and mysteries of Nature, greater are the challenges that come to his imagination. Sometimes, finding experimental support to a theoretical prediction becomes difficult. Similarly, at number of occasions finding theoretical support to experimental evidence becomes difficult. So the theory and experiment in physics are like two hands of a double-ended saw. Sometimes theoreticians lead and sometimes experimentalists pave the way but they complement each other beautifully.

It is human tendency to become a prisoner of one's experiences. So, knowingly or unknowingly, we become biased. It is a real hurdle in the journey of progress. History witnessed many such incidences. The confusion that 'the earth revolves round the sun or the sun revolves round the earth' took many years in getting resolved. Likewise, the issue that the light is a form of 'wave' or a stream of 'particles' took many years in getting settled.

Actually problem arises when we don't want to pay heed and understand the opponent's logics. We remain rigid because of our own beliefs and preconceived notions. The spirit of physics doesn't support this. Instead of becoming rigid, we should carefully listen and understand the directions and guiding principles of others' logic. We should never get biased under any circumstances and reject anybody's proposal simply because it doesn't fit in our frame. Our liking or disliking may have 'emotional value' for us but it has no value and place in physics. Ernest Rutherford's proposal of 'solar system like atom' model in place of his master's J.J. Thomson's 'water melon like atom' model is a unique example. Here with the whole hearted reverence for his mentors, he worked in favour of the spirit of physics. Actually, physics suggests that one should not take anything for granted or by its face value only. It may so happen that by proceeding logically, we may land in completely unknown and unexplored territory. If this happens, we should have confidence in our logic and need not worry about. Later in the book we will see how beautifully Clerk Maxwell developed his 'theory of electromagnetism' and predicted the electromagnetic wave nature of light. His elegant theory guided researchers and experimentalists and proved to be a turning point in physics. Similarly, Albert Einstein's logical stride in the last twentieth century transformed the very axioms of physics and triggered yet another upheaval.

Is physics difficult?

How can an exciting and interesting subject like physics always being in the logical path be difficult? But at times, we overhear from the people that physics is difficult to understand. They may, however be right. Actually, it is the attitude that makes things easy or difficult. So the mindset and perception towards it are very important. The presence of inherent fear generally stops one to undertake any adventurous journey in the world of physics. Here we can compare the condition of learner with that of a boy who is standing at the bank of a river and if pushed fearing to be drowned. But after accumulating courage and winning over the fear, he takes it head-on, learns swimming and successfully crosses the river.

Physics is a natural science and so it requires natural fascination for its understanding. In order to get firm footings and strength in the world of physics, one requires open-mindedness and inquisitiveness.

Actually a hindrance on the way in developing the logic makes physics difficult only when our mind is not trained on how to observe and listen carefully. Many of the logics in physics are expressed in the form of mathematical structures. When they appear, physics may appear dry and dull. Some feel difficulty in dealing with them at that point of time. But it should be remembered that physics is not merely mathematics. Stripped of mathematics, physics, especially at micro-level, becomes pure enchantment. It shows deep relationship with philosophy. The philosophical aspects of physics and their underlying deeper meanings attract many non-specialists to join physics stream.

Actually, 'physics' is like conventional 'language'. It has its own 'alphabets'. The letters of 'physics' are 'physical parameters' like 'length', 'mass', 'time', 'temperature', 'charge' etc. The 'meaningful words' like 'velocity', 'acceleration', 'force', 'energy', 'power' etc. are created from these letters. In physics, the words are connected together to form sentences in the form of 'equations', following certain rules defined in terms of certain natural laws and principles. Though logical in its growth, physics reaches a territory where common man's imagination doesn't work.

Physicists probe and unfold the mysteries of the universe but still there are many puzzling questions, multitudinous curiosities and challenges that are awaiting the new generation physicists to be addressed. Inquisitive mind knows no bounds. John Bardeen rightly said once that 'Science is a field which grows continuously with ever expanding frontiers'. Enrich your mind with knowledge of all the treasures created by mankind.

Let us now see how physics started evolving and the world feeling the impact and an era of transcendent as we proceed subsequently. Let us plunge deeper and deeper feel the excitement.

PART – II

PHYSICS BEGINNING TO BUILD, WORLD BEGINNING TO CHANGE

3

EVOLUTION AND TRANSITION

The experiences related to 'space' and 'time' are unique and varying. We can actually observe the real 'space' but as far as 'time' is concerned, we can only feel and sense it passing. Unlike 'space', we cannot preserve it. For us, 'time' remains eternal and so we don't bother much about its origin. But when we experience the 'motion' and its association with 'time', our inquisitive mind becomes interested in knowing the 'amount of time' that elapsed between the events. Likewise the early man started getting the ideas by noticing the occurrence of some reliable cycles of repetitive nature in the surroundings.

The early man wisely imagined by choosing the repetitive cyclic event as the basis of 'time measurement'. The cycles are associated with the change of seasons and motions of the sun, moon etc. All the periodic natural events thus became 'timekeepers' for him. Then, the idea of dividing the cyclic periods into small durations came. After this, the things became easier. The careful observations of the rising and diminishing length of the shadow of an object during the day helped him in developing a technique to measure the time. He then logically defined the time spent during two successive seasons like summer or winter as year. Similarly, he defined the time elapsed between two consecutive full-moons or new-moons as month and the time elapsed between two consecutive sunrises or sunsets as day. After this, he further divided the period of day into hours; hour into minutes and minute into seconds. He then developed 'sundial'. But in night, there is no sun. He tackled the problem quite intelligently and developed 'water', 'sand' and 'candle' clocks. All these are now the forgotten clocks. Still they are important because they teach us how ideas get generated and materialized. Today, many new types of clocks have been invented, but the underlying spirit remains unchanged.

On the 'time-front', one more development took place to benefit the society. It is about the development of the 'calendars'. The calendars are the systems of organizing units of time over an extended period to satisfy the needs of society. They provided basis for planning agricultural, religious and other civilian events. They appear truly a link between the cosmos and terrestrial life.

In the earlier phase, the sharp and watchful eyes of an inquisitive man contributed a lot. The curiosity was the main driving force to him. The 'matter' on the earth and the 'celestial objects' attracted his attention. The 'atomic theory' of matter was proposed both in India and Greece. The philosophers like Empedocles, Democritus and others in Greece and *Kanad* in India probed the matter and proposed all matters to be made of '*kana*' or 'atom' as the smallest indivisible particle of matter. The observations, intuition and imaginations were helping in creating the spectrum of knowledge.

Guidelines set

The 'fire' and 'wheel' were the most ancient discoveries brought by anonymous people. Effect of heat from 'fire' on matter is quite apparent. It helps in transforming the matter in different states. The importance of 'push' and 'pull' are known to man in displacing objects. To fulfill the need to port heavier luggage from one place to other, the idea of making 'carts' was actualized. The wheels were innovatively used in carts for easy movement which increased efficiency. The 'wheel-carts' then became a new means of transport. We can still see these carts pulled by animals even today. 'Man-pulled rickshaws' and the 'wheel barrow' are also used at some places. In this way, the 'wheel' became synonym of 'progress' and the 'fire' that of 'power'. The history of different civilizations, known through archaeological excavation, clearly indicates that 'wheel' and 'fire' always remain central in the advancement of the societies.

Thus, the guidelines were set. Discovering natural laws by observing terrestrial and celestial phenomena, understanding the matter deeply for creating new materials, innovative applications of scientific principles in creating some simple machines etc. started appearing in the agenda list of the physicists.

Scientific activities

In the beginning, the hypothesis of 'God' too helped man in finding answers to natural events. For a long period of time this hypothesis played a central role in defining physical cosmos. Initially, some religious explanations were also offered to most of the natural phenomena. But they did not work all the time. Doubting minds were always there to raise serious questions which asked for profounder hypothesis. Parallel to the religious activities, scientific activities triggered to find some logical explanations. In Greece, Aristotle contributed a lot, who believed that the observations can help in discovering the natural laws that govern the Nature. So, he promoted the concept of 'observation' before proposing any theory. This led to the birth of 'natural philosophy' in the West. It has drawn its strength from the study of Nature and of the surroundings. Since they had limited means to perform the experiments, they relied on a range of unverifiable intuitive assumptions or beliefs. These beliefs have their roots in religion and mythology. So, science and religion moved together for quite a long period.

The observations, logics and the intuition created a 'belief system'. 'Seeing is believing' became the guiding principle and powerful punch. The observations started accumulating which further added to our belief system. The faith in the beliefs has become so strong that nobody could think even to verify and prove them. That's why the beliefs that 'the sun revolves round the earth', or that 'the elements- earth, air, fire, and water- created the matter' etc. were rooted deeply and had prevailed till the15th century. With the passage of time and rising rationality, some of the beliefs were challenged. Galileo Galilei being one of them challenged the people's belief about the relationship between the falling bodies and their weight. Before Galileo, it was believed that the heavier bodies take less time in falling as compared to lighter ones. Galileo's logical mind did not agree to this. He had a doubt in his mind and so he decided to verify it experimentally. He performed the famous experiment from 'leaning tower of Pisa' and proved the prevailing belief to be wrong. He explained the logic to be incomplete because 'the motion opposed by the air present in the atmosphere' was not considered therein. This objective way of testing the prevailing beliefs brought a 'turning point' in physics. Now, only the experimentally verifiable beliefs or experiences with logical inclinations became the part of physics. Physics started growing and evolving thereafter. Enormous activities triggered.

With the progress and power of human knowledge and rising faith in rationality, the need for the unverifiable beliefs started diminishing. The science and religion started deviating from each other. Italy, Germany, England, France etc. emerged as new activity centers. The celestial and terrestrial phenomena were the major attractions, but with new visions and philosophy. Most of the scientific activities were related to the practical problems. The major impetus was on scientifically guided experiments.

The inquisitiveness of physicists to explore more about 'heavens', heavenly bodies and interiors of the objects let them go beyond the natural limits of their natural sensors for the invention of telescopes and microscopes. Soon many new secrets and interpretations emerged. Earlier, in the fifth century, *Aryabhatt* of India intuitively had proposed the idea of 'earth revolving round the sun'. But the prevailing contemporary belief did not support it. In the fifteenth century, after making careful observations of the motion of celestial bodies, Nicoleus Copernicus raised the doubt.

He proposed a theory in which not the 'earth' but the 'sun' was in the centre of the universe. Galileo appreciated the theory and started collecting evidences in support. He invented a telescope and observed the craters on moon and the moons of Jupiter. Observation of these moons was very important discovery as it provided a proof that not all the objects in the sky are revolving round the earth as per prevailing belief. His contemporary Johannes Kepler observed and studied the trajectories of planets. He found that the orbits of the planets are elliptical in nature and during motion, their angular momentum remains conserved. From these, he immediately got an explanation to the observed variations in the orbital velocity and time periods of the planets. He summarized his observations and analysis in the form of 'laws of planetary motion'. With these discoveries, a gradual shift from the 'geo-centric' universe to 'sun-centric' took place. The astronomers' painstaking discoveries brought a paradigm shift and the world witnessed the birth of a 'scientific revolution' in Europe! Its effect started diffusing slowly and steadily ultimately spread covering the entire globe.

Physicists made some keen observations and got new clues to develop understanding and to create many new ideas. The ideas were then used to develop logical theories. The experiences and observations are usually expressed in terms of 'equations' and 'formulas' in the theories. This is essentially an 'economic' way of expressing the experiences gained with the appropriate use of mathematical tools. Thus the theories and models not only explained the 'observed one' but made many predictions too. Each theory covered wide area of activities. But the theories were not final. They were put to test with every new observation. When the existing theory didn't work, refinements were made to make it better. But when the refined theory also didn't work, the wheels were reinvented in order to create new theory on new foundations.

The impact of objective approach was clearly visible when Isaac Newton arrived with his master stroke and vision. He brought a sea change in systematizing the scientific knowledge. He experimented and explored different types of motions and discovered the governing 'natural' laws. According to an anecdote, Newton was so curious and excited to know about the gravitational attraction after he saw an apple falling down from a tree. He discovered the 'laws of gravitation' and found first 'constant' of Nature in the form of the universal gravitational constant (G). Then he concentrated on the 'terrestrial motions' and found two important secrets of nature. The first one was related to 'inertia' (i.e. property of any object to remain in its own state of motion) and the second was associated with the inherent 'action-reaction' behaviour of the bodies (i.e. any action performed by a body on another is countered by equal and opposite reaction). He further observed that an 'external force' is required to change the state of motion of the body. The force brings change in the motion of the body by bringing change in its velocity, whose rate depends inversely on the body's mass. Newton finally succeeded in expressing his experiences and analysis in the form of 'three laws' that govern all kinds of motion. These 'laws of motion' ultimately led to the foundation of contemporary physics, the so called 'classical physics' of today. These laws helped in developing the theories to explain different phenomena. They were found to be quite useful and tenable. Newton found that apparently different looking celestial and terrestrial motions could be explained by this single set of laws. Thus Newton paved the way to move towards unification.

Our everyday sensory experience is related to sound. Soon, it was recognized as produced by the 'vibrational motion' of the bodies. While understanding the propagation, its 'wave nature' emerged. Newton's laws were employed successfully to understand sound and the 'physics of waves' was created.

Further, our daily life experiences related to the thermal phenomena helped in discovering many new secrets of Nature. These were related to heat transfer and energy conversion. Physicists realized that in any process the total energy remained conserved. It could neither be created nor destroyed. However, it might be changed from one form to another. A relationship was discovered between work and heat by James Prescott Joule. The physicists like Rudolf Clausius and Lord Kelvin put their experiences logically in the form of a law, known as 'second law of thermodynamics'. According to this, a part of the energy always goes as a 'waste' in the form of heat and so 100 % efficiency is unattainable. This made the fact clear that creating perpetual-motion machines (i.e. those machines that once started continue working without any external supply of energy) is impossible. The experience further led physicists to understand the direction of flow of heat and the 'order' that existed in Nature. It is not the 'quantity' but the 'quality' of heat that governs the heat flow from one body to another. Further, the natural direction of heat flow and occurrence of other natural events were also understood in terms of 'orderliness of the state of the systems'. We know that it is natural to go from 'ordered state' to 'disordered state' but not otherwise. A new term 'entropy was coined to measure the 'degree' of order. All these experiences were embodied in the form of 'laws of thermodynamics'. The base of classical physics got further broadened, when 'heat' was found to be related with the internal motions of the constituents of matter. The concept prevailed till the beginning of the twentieth century. After this, a revolutionary change came in the very thinking itself at conceptual level. It is due to the pioneering work of Albert Einstein, which made 'mass' and 'energy' equivalent. Thus, it is not only the energy of the system but the combined 'energy and mass' that remains conserved during any process. Truly, a revolutionary change in the very understanding with unimaginable consequences! We will come on this later subsequently. This time, let us pay little more attention on how the new world-view was created.

The understanding of the macro-world achieved through physical laws was amazing. The vast universe started appearing like a collection of physical bodies moving through space according to certain physical laws expressed in mathematical language. The success achieved so far made contemporary physicists so confident that they didn't hesitate in making bold statement like 'all aspects of Nature could be formulated in terms of these laws' and 'the laws and mathematical expression of Nature are the only truths'. During the course of journey, scientists made many observations and had many experiences. But all that could not qualify to become a part of science. This science included only those experiences which were common and having objective values. Many of the experiences that were purely 'subjective' in Nature could not qualify to be 'scientific'. The selection of objective observations and experiences from all is analogous of taking a 'common factor' from the given algebraic terms present in a mathematical expression. The 'common factor' is what makes 'science', leaving aside the terms in the bracket. Thus, many important experiences that may deeply be related to science were sidelined from the scientific stream. In the words of Galileo 'tastes, odours, colours, and so on are no more than mere names so far as the object in which we place them is concerned, and... they reside only in the consciousness'. The physics started working with the 'objective world-view'. Newton and his contemporaries' contributed a lot. The universe started appearing more and more like a 'machine' and operating like a 'clock'. So, it is 'predictable', 'certain' and 'deterministic' world. Thus, the success of physics created this 'mechanistic world-view'.

The world had begun to change. Application of 'fire' on water had changed its 'state'. The new state, 'steam', was found to be associated with 'power'. Then the idea of 'coupling' steam with wheel came in mind to use the power advantageously. The idea worked and different models of 'steam engine' were invented. But it was 'James Watt's engine' that gave birth to the 'industrial revolution' in Europe. This was a new beginning followed by many other technological developments. Different types of machines were invented that could give the production of the things at a cheaper and the faster rate to fulfill the growing need of increasing population of the globe. Physics and its principles were in the heart of all the innovations.

In this way, physics became not only special but favourite also and started getting social recognition and acceptance. So, physics became a natural epicentre of tremendous activities. For the growth of physics, not only the experiences related to motion and heat were responsible but, those related to light also contributed.

Guidance from Light

The light has always been a source of curiosity. The properties of light coupled with different material properties were meaningfully exploited in developing devices like 'microscopes' and 'telescopes' that enhanced our capabilities to observe finer and penetrate deeper.

Many natural events related to light started attracting the attention of physicists. The miraculous appearances of occasional 'solar and lunar eclipses' and 'rainbow' in the sky made physicists curious. The 'solar eclipse' occurs when the moon comes in between the sun and the earth whereas the 'lunar eclipse' results when the earth comes in between the sun and the moon.

Newton performed many experiments on light. He found that sunlight is actually a mixture of light of different colours. He inferred this on the basis of his innovative experiments with prism. He noticed that when sunlight passed through a prism, it got dispersed into its constituent seven colored bands with red and violet as two extremes, same as found in rainbow. The secret behind the appearance of rainbow is now open. The phenomenon of 'dispersion' is behind its formation. Actually, after rain, tiny water drops appear in the atmosphere. When sunlight passes through them, rainbow appears for the time-being under some suitable conditions.

Our eyes are sensitive to the rainbow colours, and so the spectrum comprising these colours is termed as 'visible spectrum'. It's interesting. But other parts of our body experience 'heat' and not 'colours'. Is there any relationship between the colour of light and temperature? William Herschel became interested in finding the answer to this question. He studied different parts of the spectrum using thermometer. He failed to find any relationship as his thermometer didn't give any indication of this in the entire visible range of the spectrum. But he surprisingly observed that the mercury in his thermometer started rising in the region beyond red in the 'land of no-colours'. Herschel got the 'answer'. Some invisible radiations are present in the solar spectrum. Thus, he quite unexpectedly discovered heat producing radiations. These are new invisible 'infrared' radiations.

If invisible infrared radiations are found beyond the red region on one side of spectrum, some kind of invisible radiation may also be present on the other side of the spectrum i.e. beyond the violet. Scientist Johan Ritter started thinking in this direction. He wanted to know about an activity that increases while going from red to the violet side in the solar spectrum. From the researches in the field of chemistry he came to know that the 'silver halides' were light sensitive compounds and gave 'photo-induced chemical reactions'. It was known that the rate of reaction was least in the presence of red light but enhanced rates were obtained in the presence of yellow, green and blue lights. With this knowledge, he began his studies in order to explore the region beyond violet in the solar spectrum. He was surprised to note that the silver halide was affected in the region beyond violet. This clearly indicated the presence of some invisible radiation there. These radiations were named as 'ultraviolet'. In this way the 'solar spectrum' got broadened and crossed the visible limits. The 'infrared' and 'ultraviolet' radiations became new scientific tools to explore the Nature at a deeper level.

New techniques of observing the solar spectrum were developed. Reflection and transmission gratings (ruled reflecting or transmitting surface having close, equidistant, and parallel lines) were invented to study spectral properties of light. Joseph von Fraunhofer observed some mysterious 'black lines' in the continuously appearing solar spectra as if they were dividing the whole spectrum into several parts. This mysterious observation motivated him to examine other sources. Interestingly, the moon and other planets, gave similar black lines as observed in the sun but the spectra of other stars were differently exhibiting their respective characteristic features. Logical conclusion was drawn that planets and moon reflected sun light but other 'stars' like sun had their own characteristic light. The reason for the 'partitioning' was not obvious and so it proved to be quite puzzling.

Chemist Robert Wilhelm Bunsen and physicist Gustav Robert Kirchoff were interested in the study of light from the burning materials. They developed spectroscopic techniques to make such a study. Bunsen invented a burner that gave colourless flame. The flame turned yellow when sodium salt was sprinkled over it. Its spectrum showed a bright yellow line. The yellow line became an indicator of sodium. When they passed sunlight through this sodium flame, the bright yellow line turned dark. They started thinking, how the use of solar light could change the bright line into black one.

The solar light's spectrum already contained this dark line but this time, it had become darker. To find the answer, they studied flames using some other salts like that of potassium, barium, calcium etc. and confirmed the results. In all the cases, at respective locations darker lines appeared. In this way, they noticed a correspondence between the 'bright' and Fraunhofer dark lines. The secret was now open. They inferred that Fraunhofer lines were created in the solar spectrum when white light from the core of the sun was absorbed by the atoms present in solar atmosphere. When this light is passed through the flame, additional sodium atoms absorbing more light make the corresponding line darker.

The two situations discussed above naturally arise under 'total solar eclipse' and 'no-eclipse' periods. Under 'no-eclipse' conditions, the sun is present but under 'eclipse' conditions the sun is hidden. However in both the conditions, the atoms are present. They noticed that all the black lines mysteriously appearing under 'no-eclipse' condition appeared as bright lines under 'eclipse' conditions. Thus a relationship between the light emitted from the sun and the presence of the light absorbing or emitting atoms in the solar environment was discovered. On comparing the results, it was found that in both the cases, the same atoms were involved. The origin of Fraunhofer's black lines is no longer a puzzle now. The above work led scientists to think that materials could be identified by their unique properties of selective absorptive or emissive properties of the atoms. Actually the atomic spectra are like 'fingerprints' comprising a set of spectral lines. The characteristic lines present in the spectrum are actually the 'signatures' of the atoms, the smallest chemically important part of the matter. It opened a new 'window' to study the universe.

Physicists now started studying the optical properties of the terrestrial materials in order to know the signatures to recognize the 'basic elements' responsible for creating diverse materials at such a large scale. They observed that a special set of spectral lines (like our fingerprints) was associated with a particular type of element. As each spectral fingerprint represented one element, it became easy to recognize the basic elements. Further, this also provided a hint on the presence of mysterious internal structure of matter. This type of inference was also drawn when the elements were studied with chemical point of view. The elements exhibited periodic properties and were observed to form groups. They were arranged by Dmitri Mendeleev in a table called 'periodic table'. The basis of arrangement was 'atomic weight'. Initially there were some empty places (gaps) in the table. His faith in the symmetry was so strong that he predicted the existence of the elements like germanium, manganese, scandium, gallium etc. to fill the gaps. In due course of time, these elements were discovered and the gaps were filled. Today, we know the number of naturally existing elements as 92.

The physicists were elated by the successes they had in decoding the meaning hidden in light signal. They were now contemplating to know much more about the constitution of stars and also about the material properties. For this, the physicists started analyzing the light coming from the stars. They were happy to learn that the non-terrestrial bodies like sun were found to contain the same kind of terrestrial materials. By recognizing and analyzing the signatures of elements they could unfold the mystery that the material constituting the universe is same!

Meanwhile, Joseph Stefan and Ludwig Boltzmann showed that the rate of the energy emitted by the 'black body' (an idealized body that is the perfect absorber and looks black when cold) was related to its temperature. Wilhelm Wien found that the distribution of energy had certain maxima corresponding to certain wavelength. This position depended on the temperature of the black body. These researches provided new keys to understand stellar features. Thus, spectra also helped them to estimate the 'temperature' of the stellar bodies. Later, we will see that the meticulous analysis of light helped us in knowing the answer to the age-old problem related to the origin of universe. Right now, let us look into another aspect of light that is related to its nature.

The debate about the nature of light dates back to the seventeen century. Newton believed that the light is made of tiny particles 'corpuscles' while Christian Huygens believed it to possess 'wave' nature. The then evidences were inconclusive. The debate settled in favour of 'wave' nature in the nineteenth century when Thomas Young, doctor by profession, but deeply interested in science, demonstrated the phenomena of 'interference' through his famous 'double slit experiment'. Getting interference from light was not an easy task as for this two superimposing coherent waves (i.e. having constant phase difference) are required. These cannot be obtained from two different light sources as the phase difference between the waves so obtained never remains constant. It is at this point, Young got an idea of getting two coherent light waves from the wavefront spreading out from a point source. For this, Young took a narrow light beam from a point source and passed it through two closely spaced narrow slits. He then allowed the coherent beams so obtained to interfere and used a screen to observe the resulting pattern. To his great surprise, he saw that the 'light' plus 'light' produced not only the expected 'brighter light' but also created the 'darkness' in the pattern. Young could immediately understand the reason behind. The pattern resulted because the light behaved like 'wave' and not like 'corpuscle'. Two 'out of phase' waves on reaching at a location, get superimposed over each other producing darkness, whereas 'in-phase waves produce the opposite effect i.e. brightness at that location.

At that time Young, like Huygens, believed the light waves to be 'longitudinal' like sound waves propagating in gases or liquids. They may however be transverse too. The issue got resolved after the discovery of Étienne-Louis Malus on the polarizing capability of light. He surprisingly noted the variation of the intensity in the reflected light of the setting sun by viewing it through rotating crystal of 'Iceland Spar'. He observed the same effect when he studied the light scattered through many other substances. This observation of direction-dependence of light intensity or technically lack of symmetry about the direction of propagation is possible only if the light waves are 'transverse' and not 'longitudinal'. Thus, the polarizing ability of light established light wave to be of 'transverse' nature. But, still what makes it transverse was not clear. So, the search continued. The centre of attention was the medium through which light waves propagate. Actually the longitudinal waves cannot be polarized.

Huygens while proposing his 'wave theory of light' hypothesized the presence of all pervading medium 'ether' in the space. The belief in the presence of ether was the need of the theory as a wave needs a medium to propagate. Though after the discovery of interference and polarization, the hypothesis was convincing, but the direct experimental evidence of ether was required to provide a solid base to the wave theory. For experimentalists, it was not an easy task. Physicists thought this problem to be of more academic interest and so it lost immediate priority from the agenda. The scientists concentrated their attention on the studies of materials and their properties.

There are certain materials that exhibited magnetic properties. The natural 'loadstone' has been found to attract iron needle. Further the loadstone, when suspended freely, has been found to rest in north-south direction. This observation found immediate application in navigation and in locating exact north. It led to the invention of magnetic compass. With the point of view of physics, the work in magnetism was initiated by William Gilbert who explained the behaviour of 'loadstone' by proposing earth to behave like a 'magnet'.

One more area of great interest that always remained a centre of attraction was that of 'electricity'. The man was familiar with electricity since ages. Ancient people were aware of the fact that some objects, such as rods of amber, when rubbed with cat's fur got 'charged' and developed a 'capability to attract' light objects like feathers. But they were unable to understand its mechanism. Charles Augustin de Coulomb tried to quantify the resulting force and discovered certain laws. The force between the charges increases with the increasing magnitude of the charge and show inverse square dependence on the separation between the charges. But much new was not coming up.

The renewed interest in the area of electricity was seen after Benjamin Franklin's courageous experiments on 'atmospheric electricity'. He flew a kite in raining sky and attached a metal key at the end of the moist string. He surprisingly noted sparks jumping from the key to his hand during 'lightening'. This was demonstrating the occurrence of an electrical event especially when positive charge met negative charge. He immediately inferred lightening to be electrical in nature and capable of passing the charge from the atmosphere to the ground through his body! One more event that brought revolutionary change was related with Alessandro Volta's discovery. Volta got impressed by the work of biologist Luigi Galvani but doubted on the conclusions. Galvani while doing his experiment on frog observed that the leg of the impaled frog in contact with brass hook, contracted on coming in contact with an iron scalpel. He attributed this to the presence of electricity in the frog's body and thus claimed to discover 'animal electricity'.

After the discoveries of 'atmospheric' and 'animal' electricity, there appeared a sudden upsurge in the activities in the field of 'electricity'.

New inventions: New attractions

Volta was not convinced with Galvani's proposition of 'animal electricity'. He performed many experiments and showed that any moist or porous material like cotton kept between two dissimilar metals would produce the same effect as observed by Galvani. Thus, according to Volta, Galvani's observation had nothing to do with animals. It was a pure 'chemical effect'. The Volta's work paved the way of developing a 'steady source of electricity'. Volta himself developed a 'pile' known after his name as a source of electric current. In today's technical terminology it is called 'battery'. It stores electrical energy in the form of chemical energy. The electric current flows in the closed electric circuit with battery.

Hans Christian Oersted started studying the effects of passing electricity (i.e. electric current) in the solid materials from the battery. In an experiment, he observed an interesting effect. According to this, the current carrying metallic wires could influence the magnetic compass. André-Marie Ampère gave quantitative description of 'Oersted effect' in the form of a 'law', known after his name. Michael Faraday also got impressed with 'Oersted effect'. Immediately, Newton's laws of motion came in his mind. If current carrying conductor can exert a force on magnet of the compass then it should also exert an equal and opposite force on the current carrying wire. He realized the idea and successfully demonstrated that the 'current carrying conductor' really experiences a 'mechanical force' when placed in the magnetic field. This was amazing as it showed that electrical energy is not only converting into magnetic energy but also into mechanical energy. Keeping in mind 'Oersted effect', he further started thinking that if magnetism could be obtained from electricity then why not to look into the other possibility i.e. to get electricity from magnetism. He tried in many ways but failed. Finally, he discovered that electric current can flow in a closed metallic loop only if it moves relative to magnet. The effect is not observed if the 'relative motion' becomes nonexistent. This implies that it is the energy associated with motion (i.e. mechanical energy) is getting converted into electrical energy.

These were revolutionary discoveries, which provided a new ground for technological innovations. When techniques of getting electricity from mechanical energy and mechanical energy from electrical energy were discovered, new ideas of technological importance took birth. The 'sound' is a form of 'mechanical' energy. Using these principles, the conversion of 'sound' into 'electrical' and getting it back as 'sound' was innovatively achieved. The technological innovations resulted in the discoveries of 'loud speakers' and 'microphones'. Soon the techniques to record sound signals were discovered. These recordings were used in the 'gramophones' (in which a metallic needle mechanically vibrates according to the sound track of the moving record) to get original recorded sound back at any desired time. The impact of these discoveries was clearly visible in the life style of the then society.

Another successful idea of getting mechanical energy from electrical was innovatively used in order to invent 'electric motors'. Faraday's idea of getting electrical energy from mechanical energy resulted in inventing the electric dynamos. In dynamo, the conductor is rotated in steady magnetic field. The power required to keep conductor moving was obtained from some external source like water falls, wind etc. In order to develop steady electrical power sources, other methods were also tried. The 'steam power' was one of them. The possibilities of converting hydro power, wind power, tidal powers etc. in electrical power were explored and techniques were invented to make them economically viable. The principles of electricity and magnetism were applied to enrich the field of communication. The 'telegraph' and 'telephone' emerged as new electrical wired communication systems. All these discoveries influenced the social and cultural life to a great extent.

The works done in the area of electricity and magnetism revolutionized the physics by establishing the fact the electricity and magnetism were interrelated phenomena. A new subject 'electromagnetism' emerged in the field of physics. Faraday introduced a concept of the 'field' in order to understand electromagnetism. However, the idea of field was not new to physics. Newton used it while dealing with gravitation but only to get 'computational ease'. The field at any point is an additive effect of the force between all the pairs of the bodies. So, for him 'force' was fundamental and 'instantaneous action at a distance' is a reality. But Faraday's introduction of field brought a sea change in the understanding. The field remained no longer a theoretical concept now. Faraday made it a real entity. A body has gravitational field and a charge has electrical field. If a body enters in the field of another body, it creates a disturbance. This disturbance creates a wave in the medium that propagates with some finite velocity. So, the belief of 'instantaneous action at a distance' remained no longer valid now. The delayed action usually observed, can only be understood through the 'field' concept. Thus, Faraday revolutionized the then-physics by careful experimentation and his intuitive ideas. Then, there appeared one more giant physicist Clerk Maxwell in the scene.

Maxwell's elegant way

Clerk Maxwell is credited for bringing another breakthrough in physics purely by logical thought. His starting points were the then experimental results on electricity and magnetism and their expression in the form of laws. He noted that in the laws, electric and magnetic quantities appear as partial derivatives (it is a mathematical tool that measures how a function changes with respect to some specific variable, keeping other variables constant) of multi-variable functions in space and time and some constants. So, he translated all the laws in the form of a set of four 'partial differential equations' (PDE) which enabled him to use the appropriate mathematical tools. When he carefully looked at the equations, he noted incompleteness in one of the equations. He noted that the effects arising due to 'time-varying magnetic fields' are present but the effects due to the 'time-varying electric fields' are missing. It is here, he thought of incorporating these effects in the formulation. For this, Maxwell thoroughly revisited all the laws governing the phenomena of electricity and magnetism and included the ignored effect in the form of intuitive but logical 'displacement current' in his equation corresponding to Ampere's law. Then, he started amalgamating and manipulating them using 'mathematical tools'. This resulted into a well-developed new elegant electromagnetic theory. According to his theory any oscillating or accelerated charge creates a disturbance in the space that propagates in the form of 'electromagnetic waves'. The theory predicted that the 'wave velocity' should always remain constant and independent of any frame of reference. Interestingly, this comes out to be equal to that of light. It was this result that led Maxwell to speculate that light should be electromagnetic wave and transverse in nature. It was this work of Maxwell that made 'optics' as an integral part of 'electromagnetism'. In this way, the phenomena related to electricity, magnetism and light can be dealt with a single unified theory. The guidelines to decide the agenda for future course got changed now. The theorists started setting the agenda for experimentalist. So, the job of physics remained no longer limited. It was not only to explain the natural phenomena but also to predict what can logically be possible. Physics came in a role to add into what naturally exists.

Hendrik Antoon Lorentz made many other significant contributions which were done by remaining in the influence of Maxwell's theory of electromagnetism and light. He gave a very important suggestion that an atom might consist of charged particles. The electromagnetic wave in the form of light is produced when the charges present in the atom oscillate. This idea has become a new 'lighthouse' and provided necessary clues to understand many new experimental findings later on.

The study of light continued with varied interest. Maxwell's theory was so elegant and logical that there were no doubts in its predictions. So, the theory was inviting experimental physicists to get them verified. Heinrich Hertz successfully produced electromagnetic waves in the laboratory. The Hertz waves were in long wavelength region. Soon, this became the new centre of activities. Deep interest of physicists led them to make many remarkable and wonderful discoveries. Jagdish Chandra Bose and Guglielmo Marconi soon exploited their properties and developed techniques for 'wireless communication'. Signals were encoded in radio waves and were transmitted. These were then received at remote location by using a long antenna. 'Galena' (natural sulfide ore of lead) had innovatively been found suitable in detecting the signals. These new inventions and discoveries influenced each and every walk of life in a big way.

Let us go back and look at the properties of matter with electrical and electromagnetic point of view. 'Electricity' and 'magnetism' provided another versatile tool to physicists to study the matter. In addition to the magnetic effects of current, scientists observed the heating effect too. With the passage of heavy currents, the conducting wires get red-hot. During these studies, some materials were found to emit light on passing current through them. The ideas of making use of these effects came in the mind of technical people. Thomas Alva Edison was one of them who invented the 'electric bulb' that greatly influenced the society.

Physicists had also observed that electricity doesn't pass through some solids (especially nonmetals like wood, glass etc.) and liquids (coconut oil, groundnut oil etc.), but it easily passed through some substances. This led them to classify matter as good and bad conductors. Interestingly, the solid crystals of blue vitriol, common salt, caustic soda etc. are bad conductors but their solutions are not. This led to the discovery of 'electrolysis'. In this process, material from 'anode' (positively charged electrode) is deposited on 'cathode' (negatively charged electrode) kept in the suitable electrolytic solution, on passing electric current. Faraday discovered the laws governing the process. 'Electrolysis' is found to be very useful for providing a coat of gold, silver, nickel or copper on the containers or ornaments made from ordinary metals. So, the outcome of this research is well received by the people.

The gases are electrical insulators at normal temperature and pressure but at low pressures, they may not. Physicists studied the effect of electricity in gases under low-pressures and observed electric conduction. The study of electrical conduction in gases provided a new technological outlet. Physicists found it useful in developing new kind of fluorescent lamps and sodium lamp like light sources. The phenomenon of passage of electricity through gases is technically known as 'electrical discharge'.

Paradigm shift in thinking and perception

With the invention of first scientific tool, the idea to change the physical world came in the mind of scientists. With the passage of time, the first tool helped in creating many other efficient tools. With each new tool, the world started getting new shape and the society started getting new cultural and civilized face. The world was at the dawn of new civilization! It could be possible because of the growth of innovative applications of science and technology, which enhanced the potential and power of man.

The discoveries and inventions of this period started shaking the age-old foundation of life-style and thinking. The long beliefs, dogmatic faiths and many pre-conceived notions prevailing in the society, were questioned. The science started building up in logical way with no element of subjectivity. The certainty in prediction and confidence in determination led people to think in a 'mechanistic way'.

With the emergence of laws of motion, thermodynamic laws and Maxwell's equations of electromagnetism, the

Nature appeared to be much easier to comprehend. The then physicists were happy as they believed that they had found all the keys to unlock the Nature's secrets. The universe in their eyes had become no more than a huge machine with different locks at different points. The top-down i.e. reductionist's approach had become the scientific approach to solve any problem. This influenced almost all areas of human activities. A mechanistic world view emerged!

PART –III

New insight! New vision

4

MAGIC YEARS! NEW INSIGHTS!

Mechanistic way of looking at Nature led the physicists to understand the macro-world quite successfully. Different laws governing the Nature and natural phenomena were discovered and the theories were developed that formed contemporary physics. This physics, however, was unable to understand some of puzzling observations made during that period while studying the interaction of light with matter. However one thing was clear in the mind of physicists that the puzzling results were coming from the 'micro-world' and not from the 'macro-world'. So, they diverted their attention towards this unexplored part of the world. But unlike macro-world, the study of micro-world was not so simple. Atoms comprising this world were so small that their behaviour could not be studied using 'optical microscopes'. But the physicists were confident of getting answers and so, they continued taking keen interest in the clues emerging from this world. They were looking for some unexplored relationships. For this, they analyzed the spectra of light emitted or absorbed by the substances and also studied the discharge through gases under different conditions.

The physicists involved in the study of 'ionized gases' found that they behave quite differently than unionized gases. Though macroscopically neutral, it is quasi-neutral microscopically. It showed collective behaviour, and is categorized as 'fourth state of matter', called 'plasma'. Plasma is 'diamagnetic' in nature. So, it can be confined in torus like structures surrounded by strong magnetic fields. Hot and dense plasma kept in these geometries shows a great probability to undergo fusion reaction in which lighter nuclei get fused into heavier nuclei. During fusion, small amount of mass gets converted into energy. It is here physicists and technologists got interested. The energy is the need of the hour, as the world is facing energy crisis. This is the reason that with international cooperation, physicists and technologists are working on a project ITER (International Thermonuclear Experimental Reactor) to build fusion power plant. Today, plasma is really a very important area of activity.

Let us have a quick look at the developments which helped in exploring micro-world.

Hot black bodies and spectra

Physicists who were interested in the studies of thermal properties of matter observed that hot bodies emit energy in the form of electromagnetic radiation. The amount of energy radiated from the bodies depends on their temperature. Interestingly, they observed that slight increase in temperature of the body causes enormous rise in the radiated power. The spectral studies showed that the emission from the radiating hot bodies is distributed over entire spectral region.

The then successful Maxwell's electromagnetic theory suggested that these radiations must be associated with the oscillating tiny charged particle, in a manner similar to that of production of ripples at the water surface, by wiggling a finger to and fro through it. It predicted that the radiated energy should increase with increasing frequency contrary to what had actually been observed. The experimental results showed a 'peak' in the spectrum falling out to zero on either side. None of the theories could explain all the features of the black body spectrum. It was quite puzzling.

Atoms and the line spectra

The smallest particle of the elements important from chemical point of view is 'atom'. The 'atom' is an age-old concept associated with matter. Before the nineteenth century, the concept of atom had existed but only on 'philosophical' plane with very little scientific contents. In India and Greece, philosophers could intuitively speculate the presence of atom as being the smallest constituent of matter. The concept of atom was scientifically evolved during the 19th century by the seed work of John Dalton. It was further enriched by the works of Amedeo Avogadro, J.L. Prout, J.L. Gay Lussac, P.L. Dulong and A.T. Petit, Stanislao Cannizzaro and D. I. Mendeleev. All the developments took place around Dalton's atom. Actually, these works provided a large number of finer clues that helped a lot in order to understand the matter and Nature.

The physicists found that an atom absorbs or emits not the light of all frequencies but only few selected one. That's why the atomic spectrum consists of dark or bright lines (line spectrum). But when looked in the light of Maxwell's theory, the origin of the spectrum appeared mysterious. According to Maxwell's theory 'continuous' spectrum and not the line spectrum was expected. On analyzing the atomic spectrum of hydrogen, Johann Jacob Balmer and other physicists found quite surprisingly that the origin of the spectral lines follow an 'empirical regularity' in a natural way. Yes, their origin could be expressed using a mathematical series comprising of whole numbers! This provided a new clue but the direction was not clear. The understanding of atomic spectra was posing a serious challenge to the contemporary physicists.

Photo electric effect

As we have seen earlier that Heinrich Hertz performed a great experiment and provided experimental support to Maxwell's theory. While working with his radio receiver (spark gap generator), he made an interesting observation. He found that the sensitivity of the devise could be increased by illuminating it with light. Research later showed that the increased sensitivity is caused by the presence of some 'extra' electrons that are being pushed by light from the cathode of the radio receiver. This photo-induced electron emission is referred to as 'photo electric effect'. Hertz thoroughly investigated the effect and found that any type of light will not produce this effect. It is observed only when the light used to shine the metallic surface is of a value greater than certain 'critical frequency'. With this light, the 'effect' is observed even if the intensity is negligibly small. But for the light below this frequency, no matter how much intensity one puts, effect is not observed. He further noted that the value of this critical frequency depends on the nature of material of the cathode.

The observation of photo electric effect only above certain critical frequency was puzzling and was not in line with what may be expected on the basis of Maxwell's theory.

Some puzzling accidental discoveries

The end of the nineteenth century witnessed many surprises in the scientific field. Few discoveries like 'x-rays' and 'radioactivity' were made accidentally by those physicists who were involved in doing their routine works. Let us have a brief look at them first.

Discovery of X-rays

Wilhelm Conrad Röntgen accidently discovered 'x-rays' while studying cathode rays. Actually on the advice of his teacher August Kundt, Röntgen chose his career in physics. He got interested in studying the properties of cathode rays in detail. On one fine evening, he found that a barium platino-cyanide coated paper-plate, which was kept in the corner of his laboratory, suddenly started fluorescing. Röntgen got surprised as there was complete darkness in the laboratory and the cathode ray producing tube was also thickly covered. So, he could immediately guess that surely some unknown kind of new rays were being emitted from the tube and reaching up to the plate. It made him very curious. He started investigating the penetrating behavior of these rays. He got amazed when he observed that these rays could pass even through the flash of the body. However, they were unable to penetrate the bones. It's this special property which made x-rays a diagnostic tool in the medical field to detect bone fractures. As the nature of these rays was not known at that time, these accidentally discovered rays were given the name 'x-rays'. Further experiments showed that unlike cathode rays, these were not affected by electrical or magnetic fields. But as far as origin of x-rays is concerned, it looked mysterious. No clue was available which could give even a slightest hint. The x-rays were attracting the attention because of their immediate applied value. X-rays, thus, has emerged as a new area of activity.

Radioactivity

We have seen earlier that the study of interaction of light with matter gave many interesting but puzzling results. Materials were found to absorb light and were then found to emit. Though these processes are significantly very fast but in some cases, the emission is observed to be very slow. This slow emission is termed as 'phosphorescence'. Physicists were deeply involved in collecting experimental data to understand the luminescent properties of materials in greater details. Antoine Henry Becquerel was one of them. He was interested in studying uranium containing mineral 'pitch blend'. For his experiments, he used to give exposure to sunlight and then detect emission by placing it on a photographic plate. As per his anticipation, the ore produced its image. The x-rays were discovered before few months, so he believed that the effect on the plate was probably due to the emission of x-rays by the ore. Suddenly the weather changed and the sun disappeared. So he had to put off the work for few days. He then kept the ore sample along with the packet containing unexposed photographic plates in a closed drawer. When the sky got cleared, he restarted the work. He got surprised to notice that the sample had left an image on all the photographic plates in the packet. How could this happen? Was it because of uranium's mysterious behaviour? Could uranium be involved in some kind of self-emission to produce the image of sample was a moot question before him. He repeated the experiment and cleared all doubts before the announcement of this new discovery.

In this way, Becquerel discovered mysterious type of self-emission in the form of certain kind of rays from pitch blend. These rays were named as 'radioactive rays' and the phenomenon is termed 'radioactivity'. The 'radioactive rays' are of three types, of whom the two, 'alpha' and 'beta', are affected by electric and magnetic fields. But the third one, 'gamma' rays discovered later by Paul Villard, remained unaffected by them.

Though looking mysterious, the discovery of radioactivity reminded the old unexplained observation in which even a highly insulated 'electroscope' (electrical instrument used to detect the electric charge on a body) used to get discharged in the air, as if charges are present in air to make it conducting. The cause of discharge was initially thought to have 'terrestrial origin'. The discovery of radioactivity supported this belief. So, the natural radioactivity present in soil appeared as the probable answer. The scientists started testing the validity.

Believing the 'cause of discharge of electroscopes to be the 'natural radioactivity' present in the soil, physicists started performing the experiments in mines, sea, mountains etc. But discharge rates were found to be unaffected. Then balloons were tried. Interestingly, keeping in mind the terrestrial origin, an exponential decrease was expected with increasing altitude. But the initial results didn't show this variation. For about 3 kilometers, it maintained constant ionization rate and so no fall in the discharge rate. Then with advancement in technology, it was possible to collect data up to a height of about 5 kilometers. The data clearly indicated the rise in the rate with height. It was against what was expected. Naturally, 'something' is coming from the 'outer' space that seemed to be responsible for the presence of 'extra' charges in the atmosphere. This 'something' coming from outer space, making extra charges available here, is called 'cosmic rays'. Physicist Victor Franz Hess was credited for this idea and discovery. In this way, we see that though we started with radioactivity in search of an answer of the age-old puzzling problem associated with the 'discharge of electroscopes', we ended up with an entirely new answer and discovered 'cosmic rays'. The 'cosmic rays', in addition to the 'radioactivity', emerged as a new area of activity.

The origin of radioactivity was proving to be puzzling. But keeping this aside, physicists thought of studying the properties of emitted radiations in greater detail. All the three types of radioactive rays were found to be capable of producing ionization in the air. The alpha particles constituting alpha rays have been found to be massive and positively charged whereas the beta particles constituting beta rays are comparatively much lighter and negatively charged. Ernest Rutherford and Frederick Soddy found that the chemical nature of the material gets changed after the emission of alpha or beta particle. So, the radioactivity is found to create chemically different new material! Further, it is also noticed that the alpha particles have tremendous velocities and very long range. This suggested Rutherford to use them in probing the 'interior of atom' which was needed, especially after the discovery of 'electron' by J.J. Thomson.

Discovery of Electron!

As we have seen that the last decade of nineteenth century was a 'period of great unrest' in the scientific world. The reason being, the great difficulty that scientific community was facing in dealing with some puzzling observations like black body spectrum and photoelectric effect including radioactivity and x-rays by the conventional physical laws. The physicists were striving hard to get finer clues to understand Nature at deeper level. But the traditional physics was failing in providing any meaningful help. So, some physicists like Max Planck and Albert Einstein thought to move in unconventional ways with new ideas in the hope of getting solutions. They got tremendous success and revolutionized physics. We will come on these developments soon. But before this, let us go through the works of some physicists who continued the traditional line of research related to the electrically conducting properties of matter, especially of gases and discovered a 'key' to understand the properties of matter deeply.

It was the period, when Physicists developed a conventional devise 'vacuum tubes' with two electrodes, anode and cathode, in order to study the electrical conduction through gases under ultra-low pressure. They observed electrical discharge and the 'glow' in the region between anode and cathode. It was clear to them that the effect is due to 'something' emitting out from the cathode, the negative pole of the applied high voltage. Physicist J.J. Thomson got interested in knowing what exactly is coming out from cathode on the application of high voltage?

An important contribution worth mentioning at this point is about the discovery of 'Lorentz force'. It states that if a charged particle moves in the presence of a combined electric and magnetic field, it will experience a force with two components. The one due to electric field in the direction of motion of the particle and the other due to magnetic field in the direction perpendicular to both the direction of motion and the magnetic field. Thus, this law suggests that the electric field can accelerate and magnetic field can direct the charged particle to move on a circular or helical trajectory. The ideas were found quite useful later during the study of radioactivity, plasma and in developing particle accelerators. But here what is important is to know that this direction, curvature and thickness of the trajectory can help us in determining the charge and mass of the particle.

Thomson measured the properties of that 'something' which constitutes cathode rays and found that it is a tiny particle which got deflected by electric and magnetic fields. Experiments showed it to possess a negative charge and a constant value of specific charge (charge to mass ratio). He further noted that the emission of this particle was independent of the nature of the material of cathode. He thus logically thought it to be the basic constituent of atom and called it 'electron'. Interestingly, it was the same particle that we had found earlier in the form of 'beta particle'. The electric charge on the electron was found to possess a minimum value that a body can acquire. So, the charge on a body is an integral multiple of this electronic charge. The magnitude of charge ('e') has been considered as one of the universal constants of Nature. The other constants, discovered earlier, are 'G' (gravitational constant) and 'c' (the velocity of light in vacuum). None of the bodies had been found to possess fractional charge that time. However, recently, elementary particles 'quarks' have been theorized to possess fractional charge in the unit of 1/3 or 2/3 of 'e'. We will come on 'quarks' later in the book. Thus, the negatively charged 'electron' was proposed as 'basic constituent' of matter and with this, Dalton's indivisible neutral atom started showing cracks. The 'atom' became a new object of research in the twentieth century.

The physicists envisaged a great potential in the 'electron'. With the bank of knowledge collected up to the nineteenth century, physicists entered in the twentieth century along with the then challenging problems, with the sole objective to enter in the micro world. A hub of activities was initiated around atom in the twentieth century. Thomson proposed 'water melon' like model for the atom. But before we go on describing the development of atomic models, let us first see how scientists enter in the 'quantum era'.

Beginning of quantum era! New directions!

As we have mentioned earlier, when conventional line of approach was not working, physicists tried some non-conventional ideas in order to understand the puzzling observations mentioned above. Let us have a look at the developments.

Planck and his magic formula

Physicist Max Planck came forward with new proposals to solve the troubling problem of black body spectrum. Before Plank, all the efforts failed to understand the nature of the spectrum. He analyzed the efforts made so far and attributed the root of the problem to lie in the very nature of the absorption or emission processes. Everyone before him had believed the processes to be continuous. So, he thought otherwise and showed that the problem could be solved by assuming the processes to be discrete. For this, he developed quantum theory and said that the black body can absorb or emit energy of all spectral type (or frequencies) but only in the form of energy packets or energy quanta. Further, in order to quantify energy in the packet, he proposed a formula known as Planck's formula. According to this, the energy in the packet of a particular spectral type is proportional to the corresponding frequency. The constant of proportionality appeared as a new constant of Nature. It is Planck's constant '*h*'. He further proposed that the probability of absorption or emission of the quanta of high energy is very low and that of low energy is very high by the black body. Now, infinite number of energy packets of varying size of energy is involved, so, he further proposed logically that the low-energy quanta involved are maximum in number where as those of high-energy are minimum. But as far as their contribution to total energy is concerned, it remains insignificant. On the contrary, the energy packets comprising of intermediate energy are moderate in number but their contribution is very significant. This non-conventional idea worked very nicely and surprisingly explained the puzzling experimental spectral curve of black body. A new secret was found in the form of Planck's formula!

Headway: Einstein's bold proposal

In order to explain the puzzling features of 'photoelectric effect', Einstein revived Newton's corpuscular theory of light and proposed that the light consists of tiny particles, whose energy is proportional to the frequency of radiation. In contrast to Planck's thinking, he proposed that not only the 'emission' but the very 'transmission' of light takes place in quantized manner. By this assumption, Einstein succeeded in explaining the photoelectric effect. He pictured the 'effect' as the outcome of an event in which the corpuscles (light particle) interact with the electron beneath metal surface. During the interaction, light quanta transfer their energy to the electron. The minimum energy is required to cross the surface barrier. When the electron comes out, it becomes free and contributes to photoelectric effect. That's why below certain 'critical frequency' (characteristic of metal used) the effect is not observed.

Now, Einstein started thinking about the success of 'electromagnetic wave theory' of light in explaining the phenomena like interference, diffraction and polarization. So, he boldly proposed the 'dual nature' of light. Light exhibits 'both' the characters. The wave-like or particle-like nature of light depends on what experimentalist is looking for. This brought experimenter at the central stage. 'Dual nature of light' was a new secret of Nature. The 'dualistic philosophy' so emerged revolutionized our thinking and became a guiding principle for future.

Einstein's Relativistic World!

After the success of Maxwell's electromagnetic wave theory of light, physicists took 'ether hypothesis' very seriously. The physicists thought that the motion of earth could provide a clue about the possible existence of ether. With this thought, the logic started working. Albert Michelson and Edward Morley thought that if two light waves, one traveling along the direction of earth's motion around the Sun and the other across it, could be made to interfere, the evidence might be collected. They designed and performed a historic flawless experiment. The apparatus was very sensitive and so they were fully confident of getting the evidence quite comfortably. But the results of their experiment failed to provide any evidence. As the wave nature of light was a contemporary reality, the result of the experiment was termed 'negative'. The strong belief in ether hypothesis motivated physicists to offer many explanations but none were satisfactory. The 'ether' was really troubling the then physicists.

Albert Einstein looked at the problem of 'ether' at fundamental level. His particle picture of light didn't need ether and so he rejected the idea of very existence of ether on logical grounds. Again a bold step! He started with the 'principle of equivalence' of physical laws in all inertial frames of reference (the frames either at rest or moving with constant velocity relative of each other) and believed in the unquestionable theoretical result on the 'absoluteness' of the velocity of light emerged from Maxwell's theory and outlined the framework of a new theory called 'special theory of relativity' to describe the motion of bodies. His revolutionary papers brought a turning point in physics.

The intuitive ideas used by Einstein and the outcome of his theoretical developments challenged the very 'axioms' of the then physics. Einstein's work rejected the beliefs of 'absolute space', 'absolute time' and 'absolute mass'. According to Einstein all are 'relative' and cannot be defined as 'absolute' quantities. By changing the frame, the change occurs in such a way that constancy of the light's velocity is always maintained. Thus, the space and time intervals are modified by the observer's motion and remain no longer the same. The theory predicted that one cannot assign absolute meaning even to 'simultaneity' as different observers may disagree as to whether one event occurs before or after, or at the same instant as another event. The observer has now become important.

Einstein's theory uncovered yet another astonishing secret of Nature. His theory predicted the 'dependence of mass on velocity' and the 'equivalence between mass and energy'. These are logical consequences of his theory and emerged as unbelievable facts and secrets of Nature. Now, the matter and energy, seemingly opposite entities, appeared as if they are two faces of the same coin. A 'new physics' emerged. According to his theory, space and time were found to be interwoven. A 'four dimensional world' comprising of 'space-time' appeared.

After developing the special theory of relativity, Einstein started reviewing the scientific developments. He noticed that as far as Maxwell's theory of electromagnetism is concerned, it needed no corrections in the light of his new results. But Newton's theory of gravitation required some corrections. If Newton's theory is to look like Maxwell's theory of electromagnetism, corrections are to be made in the energy, momentum and mass as per requirements of relativity theory. After this thought, he then examined Newton's theory and noticed that it is based on the belief of absoluteness of space and time. That's why Newton's theory predicts that whatever happens in any part of universe can be known by anybody at the same instant. However, according to his theory, this cannot be possible as no information can travel faster than light and so instant communication is not possible. It was here that Newton's theory required modification.

From the examination of Newton's theories, Einstein found exact equivalence between gravitational and inertial mass of a body. Einstein believed that this equivalence could not be 'accidental' but a fact of Nature. So, he was interested in developing a theory in which this equivalence between two types of masses becomes necessary and not emerges accidently. It is here, a beautiful thought came in his mind. He imagined a uniformly accelerated observer in zero-gravitation field. For him, all free objects would accelerate. The state of space, as noticed by the observer, is a homogeneous gravitational field. From here, he got an idea of equivalence between the uniform acceleration and homogeneous gravitation.

In the light of above string of thoughts, Einstein could intuitively visualize that acceleration might result into gravity and inertia might result from gravitational effects. In field-free space, bodies follow straight line path but it becomes curved in presence of the field. It is here he could understand the importance of geometry. He used the mathematics employed to understand curvature and incorporated his intuitive ideas in order to develop a 'general theory of relativity'. His first theory of relativity was 'special' theory because it dealt with inertial frames only. He extended the theory to include non-inertial (accelerated) frames. Now onwards, Einstein chose most uncommon and thrilling path and extended the geometrical notion of space into that of space-time.

The curvature in space-time has been predicted to exist because of the presence of a body in the space-time. More massive is the body, more is the curvature produced by it. The space-time surface would be flat if there exists nothing on it. The actual space-time in which this universe is present has many curvatures of different radii. Minute curvature exists in the vicinity of the sun as it has smaller mass as compared to other massive stars. Though the curvature is minute, but it gives its effective presence. These curvatures in space-time are actually the indications of the presence of gravitation.

How can we know about the presence of curvatures? The theory says that the light travels on the surface of space-time only. So the light coming from a distant star guided by the curvature bends while passing close to the sun. The natural conditions to verify this prediction are created during 'total solar eclipse' for a very small period of few minutes. During total solar eclipse, stars are visible in the day-time when the sun is also present. Thus, positions of the distant stars can be pictured in the day and may be compared with that when the sun is not there in the night. The difference in the data can give information about the presence of curvature. Astrophysicists Arthur Stanley Eddington and Andrew Claude de la Cherois Crommelin experimentally observed the curvature during 1919's total solar eclipse day and provided conclusive proof of the Einstein's general theory.

The experimental confirmation of the general theory of relativity changed the very course of astrophysics and provided a new vision.

New inroads through 'Electron'

Science and technology feed off one another. Science helps in building new technology and technology helps in getting new observations. New observations and new interpretations allow us to build more scientific knowledge. This knowledge helps in growing technology further to help science. Electron's discovery is a unique example. It first affected the way to look at the atom. It helped in building electronic technology that affected almost all the fields of human interest. Actually, it is the single discovery that had tremendous impact on both science and technology. Let us see some of the application-areas that have emerged and got developed after the discovery of electron.

Electronics

The discovery of electron has brought a real breakthrough. The motion of the electron in vacuum is collision-less whereas in presence of any medium, it collides with the medium's particles. This suggests that the effective velocity of the electrons in any medium is bound to be smaller than that in vacuum. The electron is a tiny particle with mass so small that the presence of gravitational field cannot be felt by it. However it can easily sense the presence of electric field in its surrounding by experiencing a force in the direction opposite to that of the field. This suggests that the particle can be accelerated or decelerated by the electric field. Further, the moving electron generates electric current which in turn produces magnetic field (Oersted effect). This suggests that the moving electron can sense the magnetic field and can be deflected by it. Thus the motion of electron can be controlled. Now, the physicists concentrated on the techniques to produce and detect them. As electrons are present in the matter, the natural source of the electron may be found in matter. The search began for those materials which may be employed to get electrons by supplying energy from outside required by them to cross the surface potential barrier. The energy may be supplied in the form of heat, light or electricity. The physicists discovered many techniques that made thermionic, photo and field emissions possible. Now the ideas to detect and control the electrons were required. For this, scientists used vacuum tubes with two and more electrodes, now known as diodes, triodes etc. These components were innovatively used to convert a.c. (alternating) power into d.c. (direct) power and also to amplify weak electrical signals. The study gave birth to 'vacuum tube electronics' which bought revolutionary changes in the field of 'telecommunication' and 'entertainment'.

World of atom!

The electron's discovery also led scientists to enter in the world of atom. With new vision and ideas, they started visualizing the type of structure an atom can possess. The presence of the electron in neutral matter logically established the presence of equal and opposite positive charge inside it. The first atomic model was proposed by J.J. Thomson in which electrons were visualized to be embedded in the sea of positive charged atomic material like black seeds in the red part of watermelon. The first criterion for the acceptable atomic model is 'stability'. But Thomson's watermelon model failed to exhibit it when known physical principles were applied. So, further probing in the interior of atom was required. Physicist Ernest Rutherford came in the scene.

As we have mentioned earlier that Rutherford got attracted by the properties of 'alpha particles'. He thought of using them to probe the interior of atom. For this, he innovatively designed an experiment. His aim was to study the scattering of alpha particles in the hope of getting some information about the mysterious interior of the atom and also to test Thomson's atom model. For this, he directed a beam of alpha particles at thin gold foil. He noted how the alpha particles got scattered from this foil. Most of the observations were as per expectations but few of them surprised him. These were related to the alpha particles that scattered quite unexpectedly at very large angle even up to 180 degrees. The results were quite puzzling but they clearly indicated that the picture of the real atom should be different than that of Thomson. Rutherford interpreted the results in terms of the presence of positively charged 'nucleus' at the centre of the atom. His results showed that the nucleus should be much smaller as compared to the size of atom. The discovery of nucleus was most revolutionary discovery of that time. Rutherford proposed a new model for atom. His model was like our solar system in which the nucleus is like the sun and the electrons are like orbiting planets. But like Thomson's model, this model also failed to exhibit stability of the atom as the orbiting electrons continuously lose energy while revolving round nucleus and finally fall in the nucleus.

Young physicist Niels Bohr then tackled this problem of stability and the atomic line spectra innovatively. His solution seems to be a result of unique combination of imagination, intuition and realizations. For stable atom, it was clear to him that the electron should not lose energy while revolving round the nucleus inside atom. In other words, some conditions were needed to be imposed that could make the electronic orbit stationary. It was here that he remembered Planck's quantum theory and intuitively applied it on 'Rutherford's model'. In this way, stable atom model emerged. In this model, the electron always maintains a separation from the nucleus. The space in between is empty. To have an idea let us imagine a magnified atom. In this atom, if we assume nucleus to be of one meter size, then the electron in the atom will be found at about 100 km away from it. Now next aim of Bohr was to explain the atomic spectral features associated with the simplest atom hydrogen. He was aware of the fact that the atomic spectra are 'line spectra' and the spectral lines are expressible in the form of 'mathematical series'. Keeping this in mind, he started developing his atom model. He based his atom model on three basic postulates. The first one is about orbital path for the electron, which is 'circular' and 'stationary' (By stationary, we mean that the orbiting electron will not lose any energy and will have a certain well-defined fixed value); second is about the quantum restriction on the values of angular momentum of the electron which gives stationary orbits and the third is about the mechanism of absorption and emission processes. In his model, each orbit is assigned a fixed energy value and is defined by a quantum number that corresponds to the energy of the orbiting electron. The orbit with minimum energy and quantum number is known as 'ground state'. All other higher energy states are known as 'excited states'. When appropriate energy is given to the atom from any external source, electron jumps from ground state to an excited state giving rise to 'absorption spectrum'. The life time of the electron in the excited state is very small and so it falls back to ground state giving rise to the 'emission spectrum'. A complete picture of functional hydrogen atom has now emerged. It met a great success in explaining the spectral features of this atom. But understanding complex atomic systems still posed a challenge. However the 'direction' to follow is now clear. We will come on these issues later in the book. At present, let us concentrate on absorption and emission processes in some more details.

Emission process: Revisited

The absorption and emission processes have thoroughly been revisited by Einstein. In general, the atoms in a system are largely populated in the ground state as it is most stable state. When the system is irradiated, the atoms absorb energy and go to the excited states. After spending some time there, atoms start coming back to the ground state by emitting spontaneously. The time is so small that even if the system is continuously exposed to light, it never gets populated in any of the excited state and so the system remains largely populated in the ground state.

Einstein noticed from the experimentally observed emissive characteristics of atoms that the excited states may have varying life-times (from milli- to nano- seconds). So, in some cases where it is sufficiently large, maximum atoms may be sent to populate that excited state. In other words, 'population inversion' may be achieved (as excited state remains populated during this process and not the usual ground state, we call it 'population inversion'). The 'inverted' population can be maintained by pumping energy by some external means (the process of populating excited state by flash light is known as 'optical pumping').

Now let us see the emission from these systems. In normal systems, atoms get de-excited randomly and so the emission is spontaneous. There is no coherence (phase co-relationship between the photons) in the emitted radiations. But in the population inverted system, we may get a special type of emission. The process of emission can be initiated by a photon, which stimulates other atoms to get de-excited to emit exact 'copies' of the initial photon maintaining the phase and direction. The radiations so obtained from the population inverted system may thus be quite different from the 'normal' (spontaneous) emission. With this background, Einstein logically proposed emission to be of two types, 'spontaneous' and 'stimulated'. The idea of stimulated emission caught the attention as it explored the possibility of getting light to be amplified in a 'pumped population inverted system'. This predicted 'amplified light' to be highly 'coherent' and 'directional' making it very powerful. Physicists created the conditions to observe the phenomenon in different ranges of electromagnetic spectrum. Charles Townes and Arthur Schawlow invented the 'Maser' (microwave amplification by stimulated emission of radiation), using ammonia gas. The phenomenon was observed in visible region after few years. Theodore Maiman, the inventor of 'Laser' (light amplification by stimulated emission of radiation), was credited for this. He used ruby crystal. Soon, many other different materials like helium-neon, carbon dioxide, liquid dyes etc. were employed. Maser and Laser have become special type of sources which are different from the well-known incandescent and fluorescent type of light sources. Today the 'laser' is widely put to many technological applications and has thus become a house-hold device. After getting the glimpses of this revolutionary work, let us go back where we have left to continue our journey to understand matter deeply.

Periodic table revisited

New discoveries like x-rays paved the way of looking at matter in different ways. The studies revealed that x-rays exhibit all the properties shown by light. Soon, it was discovered that like light waves, these rays were also electromagnetic in nature but with much higher frequencies (i.e. shorter wavelengths). Physicists placed x-rays in the invisible part of the electromagnetic spectrum after ultraviolet radiations towards higher frequency side. Interestingly, their wavelength is of the order of inter-atomic separations in the crystals. The atoms are arranged in crystals periodically. So the crystals behave like natural 'gratings' from where x-rays can be diffracted. These studies have been used in determining the crystalline and molecular structures in later years. Before proceeding further, let us briefly go through the history which helped in creating the periodic table of elements.

Let us see the developments after Dalton's proposal of atomic theory. Avogadro put forward a hypothesis. According to this, equal volumes of different gases under identical conditions of temperature and pressure contain equal number of particles (the concept of atom or molecule was not established at that time). As the weight of these gases can be measured, the weight of single particle may also be estimated. This comes out to be very small. So, the weights are compared in order to get some reasonable number. Interestingly, they appeared as simple multiple of the weight of hydrogen atom. The number so obtained is defined as a unique property of the element that is termed as 'atomic weight'. The inferences prompted William Prout to hypothesize that all elements are made of hydrogen atoms. But soon, some elements with fractional atomic weights were discovered. This observation put doubts on the hypothesis and so it was sidelined.

The chemical elements have now been identified with their respective atomic weights. Mendeleev made this a basis and planned to arrange the elements in the increasing order of their atomic weights. He noticed that the chemical properties of elements got repeated after certain period forming various groups of elements with common properties. But some anomalies were also noticed. From experiments, it was found that the atomic weight of cobalt is 58.93 and that of nickel is 58.71. So cobalt was placed after nickel while arranging in the table. But, the chemical properties were suggesting the order to be reversed. Similar was the case with argon and potassium. These were the indications that the 'atomic weight' should not be the fundamental property of the elements.

Meanwhile, indivisibility of Dalton's atom was questioned and was replaced first by Thomson's watermelon model and then by Rutherford's and Bohr's nuclear models. The discovery of X-rays provided a new tool to study characteristics properties of elements. Moseley discovered that the frequencies of certain characteristic x-rays emitted from certain chemical are proportional to the square of a number, of positive charge present in the atom. This number is equal to the number of electrons in neutral atom. Thus, it is made clear that the positive charge residing in the nucleus is not continuous but can be assigned a number termed as 'atomic number'. This 'number' is a characteristic property of the atom. A new basis of identifying an element is found. Let us recall the example of nickel and cobalt. From Moseley's work, it was noted that nickel's atomic number is 28 and that of cobalt is 27. So when the basis of building periodic table is changed, nickel and cobalt change their order and they automatically get their respective houses as expected. A new periodic table was built and the anomalies of Mendeleev's periodic table automatically got disappeared.

After these developments, Soddy made an interesting discovery while identifying the radioactive decay products. He found that though some elements are chemically indistinguishable, but they differ in their atomic weights. Being same chemically, they have same atomic number and occupy the same place in the periodic table. They were termed as 'isotopes'. Later J. J. Thomson and Francis Aston discovered isotopes of many other naturally occurring common elements. Studies showed that sample of natural chlorine has two types of atoms with atomic weights around 35 and 37. So, its atomic weight (35.46) is the average atomic weight that results from the mixture of two isotopes in the natural sample. Thus, the presence of atoms of isotopes makes the average atomic weight fractional. The atomic weights of individual isotopes are really closer to the integral multiple of hydrogen's atomic weight. With this discovery, forgotten Prout's hypothesis (which tells that the atomic weights of elements are integral multiples of the atomic weight of hydrogen) got new life and new way of looking at the matter emerged.

Back to Bohr Model…

After explaining hydrogen atom successfully, Bohr started building periodic table arranging the electrons around the nucleus in an atom. Keeping in mind the experimental observations and periodic properties of elements, he realized that an orbit could not accommodate more than certain fixed number of electrons. According to him, the first orbit could contain only two but the next 8 and so on. Moseley's work has been found to be in accordance with Bohr's theory. But Bohr failed to discover the principle that works behind this arrangement. Wolfgang Pauli studied the experimental results thoroughly and quite intelligently discovered the appropriate principle. This is known after his name as Pauli's 'exclusion principle'. According to this principle, no two electrons can occupy the same state.

Bohr model is taken with great enthusiasm by physicists. They tried to apply and extend this model to understand other hydrogen-like systems. Meanwhile, high resolution spectroscopes were developed and wealth of new experimental results started pouring in. Physicists found that 'single spectral line' appearing in the atomic spectra is not really a single line but is made of closely packed group of lines. It is termed as 'fine structure'. But the successful 'Bohr model' failed to explain this new spectral feature. So, the physicists started analyzing it critically.

Some physicists realized that this model is not tenable because it is a 'hybrid' model, which used 'classical' and 'non-classical' (quantum) ideas. However, some physicists, like Arnold Sommerfeld, were still there who were hoping to get a way out from the Bohr model. They realized that the electron's velocity inside atom was very large and so the theory required 'relativistic corrections' because at such velocities, its mass could not be treated as constant. Sommerfeld made relativistic corrections but got only partial success in explaining the 'fine structure' of hydrogen spectrum. In spite of this, it was considered an important step in the forward direction and physicists started thinking to assign some more properties to the electron in order to make atom fully comprehensible.

George Uhlenback and Samuel Goudsmit looked back at the atom model and realized that the orbiting electron may 'spin' too. They reviewed the experimental results available in the literature and noticed that by assigning electron a 'half integral quantum number' the puzzling fine structure data can be explained. However, the idea of fractional quantum number was not in line with traditional quantum thinking. Traditionally, all quantum numbers are integers and not fractions. But Uhlenback and Goudsmit noticed its mandatory appearance to fit in the experimental data; they confidently hypothesized it in the theory.

The physicists got impressed by this hypothesis and continued to follow the line set by Neils Bohr and Arnold Sommerfeld. The state of the electron in an orbit is defined by keeping in mind its energy and its motion in the orbits of different shapes and their orientations in space. The spin hypothesis of Uhlenback and Goudsmit completed the definition of the state for the electron in the atom. The 'orbital' and 'spin' motions of electron interact giving rise to 'fine structure'.

With the characteristic spin, electron became a unique entity and has appeared as a tiny magnet. The electrons have always been found to follow Pauli's principle. It means, each electron will require a separate state to be accommodated. This makes them entirely different 'community' that always remains aloof. In other words, if we have two electrons, two independent cells will be required to accommodate them. With these insights and understanding, new physics was developing.

Birth of Quantum Mechanics

The serious question before the physicists at that time was to understand what makes 'Bohr orbits' stationary? The conventional physics had no answer. So, what to do? It was the period, when physics was undergoing a transformation. New concepts like dual nature of light, energy-mass equivalence were emerging and gaining the grounds. The age-old belief in the Nature's love for symmetry was also there to guide. Interestingly, the concept of symmetry is not only limited to the geometry only but it goes much deeper. Young de Broglie sensed the symmetry between matter and energy (radiation) and proposed 'matter-wave hypothesis'. For this proposal, he got guidance from Planck's magic formula and Einstein's 'energy-mass relation'. He obtained wonder formula for the wavelength of 'matter waves' (inversely proportional to the particle's momentum) which like Planck's magic formula revolutionized the physics.

In order to understand stationary Bohr orbits using matter wave hypothesis, let us recall, how stationary waves are formed in a stretched string. The matter waves (electron waves) in an atom can produce stationary waves only when the size of the orbit is such that it gives rise to complete loops. As fractional loops cannot exist, orbits of any arbitrary sizes are not possible. Complete loops (two, three…) correspond to their respective fixed energy and so stationary nature of the Bohr's orbit remained no longer a puzzle now.

Ervin Schrödinger got impressed with de Broglie's 'matter-wave hypothesis' as wave being everyday phenomenon, easy to comprehend. Primarily, his interest was to develop a mathematical theory that can deal with the matter waves. He started with 'electron wave'. For this, he introduced physically acceptable function called 'wave function psi (ψ) in his theory. The 'ψ' corresponds to something like physical ripples on a pond. However, the physical significance of this 'psi' was not clear to him. But, he was successful in reducing atomic problems into 'boundary value problems' and was able to reproduce Bohr's results without introducing quantum numbers on *ad hoc* basis. He solved many problems and finally succeeded in giving a very important mathematical tool in the form of 'Wave Mechanics' to tackle the problems of the quantum world. The puzzling 'quantization' appeared directly from the theory that has earlier been introduced on ad-hoc basis in Bohr's theory. So, most of the physicists got influenced by the elegance of this newly emerged Schrödinger's wave mechanics. It looked revolutionary and promising.

The wave function 'psi' employed by Schrödinger is physically well-behaved function. Max Born later interpreted this function in terms of probability of occurrence of the system in a particular state. Actually, the wave function includes all possible states in which system is likely to go giving total probability 'one'. When one solves Schrödinger equation, he gets eigen (proper) values with different probabilities. The eigen values are the values found when actual measurements are made on the system. Thus, the theory has become mathematical tool to reach at logical meaningful measurable results.

It was the period, when all thinking and new ideas were growing around Bohr's model. Influenced by Bohr and the way he explained the emission and absorption processes, Werner Heisenberg thought of following an entirely new approach. He realized that though the Bohr's orbital picture of atom was visualizable but not verifiable. In his eyes, the 'transition' should be the ideal starting point as it resulted into the experimentally observed spectrum. It was clear to him that as transition involved a pair of states, so new mathematics would be required. For this, he arranged the states in tabular form and intensively worked to discover new rules needed to develop required mathematics. In the effort, he discovered 'matrix mechanics' to handle the micro-world. He got all the results that Bohr got earlier. He was happy to note that mathematics was naturally guiding and predicting and it required no more any modeling or visualization that brings limitations in thinking and restricts imaginations.

In this way, two approaches were followed to deal with micro-world. Both looked opposite to each other but interestingly giving the same results. Schrödinger looked at the Heisenberg's approach and compared it with that of his own and demonstrated that they are actually equivalent.

Now, one more twist came in the theoretical understanding of micro-world. It came when P. A. M. Dirac, a student of Applied Mathematics appeared in the scene. It's the lecture on 'matrix mechanics' by Heisenberg that inspired him to choose this subject for his research. He got impressed and being a student of mathematics, reworked what Heisenberg had discovered on his own. He was surprised to note that his approach was simple and straight forward which made the so-called new mechanics as a special case of the familiar 'classical mechanics'.

All these theoretical developments came under one umbrella 'quantum mechanics'. In quantum mechanics, the classical dynamical variables like position, momentum, energy are replaced by their mathematical analogues 'operators' and the state of the quantum mechanical system is represented by the wave function 'psi'. When the operator is operated over the state of the system, we get the eigen value, an experimentally observable value for the system.

For micro-world, Heisenberg discovered a new rule of the game. This is 'uncertainty principle'. This applies on any pair comprising of two 'conjugate parameters' whose product gives the dimensions of 'action'. The 'position–momentum', 'energy–time' etc. are such pairs. According to this, both the quantities of the pair cannot be measured simultaneously. Say for example, if one measures position very precisely, there appears a lot of uncertainty in the measurement of momentum. Similarly, if one measures energy of the electron in any state of the atom very accurately, uncertainty in the measurement of its life-time of the electron in that state becomes very large. The ideas can also be applied for the interacting quantum systems too. A large uncertainty in the energy exchanges is possible during interaction but only for a very short period of time. However, the small energy exchanges are possible during interaction for long periods.

The 'uncertainty principle' can also be interpreted in another meaningful way. The 'position–momentum' uncertainty physically gives rise to a 'reaction' that opposes the very 'confinement' of the quantum system. In case of atom, this natural 'reaction' associated with the electron stops it from falling in the nucleus! As an illustration, let us consider an electron in the atom that is confined in a very small space of dimensions about 100 millionth of a centimeter. This gives rise to a large uncertainty in the momentum of its electron. Calculations show that electron's speed near this confinement is about 950km/s. Similarly for the proton confined in the nuclear dimensions, the speed comes out to be 65000 km/s. This suggests that the matter is highly 'dynamic' at deeper level! It is so dynamic that the one cannot ignore the relativistic effects! Remarkable work is done by Dirac. His relativistic quantum mechanical theory not only explained all the spectral features associated with the atom but also predicted the presence of 'antimatter' in the universe. This is quite surprisingly and provided a new clue to understand Nature. The theory implied that for every particle, there must be a corresponding antiparticle. For example, the antiparticle of electron is 'anti-electron' (it is now known as 'positron'). His theory also showed that the mysterious Uhlenback and Goudsmit's 'spin' hypothesized earlier is actually a 'relativistic' effect and has nothing to do with the classical mechanical top like familiar spin.

Emergence of QED

Though Quantum Mechanics met brilliant success but it was still facing some problems. The theory didn't compete with relativity as it did not include the possibility of 'annihilation' and 'creation' of particles. According to the theory of relativity, the photon of appropriate energy can create particle-antiparticle pair and particle can annihilate with its antiparticle during collision giving rise to equivalent amount of energy. So, inclusion of these possibilities while dealing with quantum mechanical systems was felt necessary. The physicists like Richard Feynman, Freeman Dyson, Sin Itero Tomonaga and Julian Schwinger tried and discovered Quantum Electrodynamics (QED). In this theory, the matter and energy both were placed at par. Actually speaking, QED is generalized version of quantum mechanical theory to deal with both 'electron' (material particle) and 'photon' (electromagnetic field particle).

The emergence of QED has provided a new understanding and new interpretations. The so called 'vacuum' is now the 'zero-field state' (i.e. the lowest energy state) of the quantized electromagnetic field in QED. The energy-time uncertainty relation working at quantum level allows the 'borrowing' of large energies from the 'vacuum' to generate 'particles' for short times. But the position-momentum uncertainty relation cannot allow these particles to stay at a fixed location with zero momentum. This is very interesting situation as it gives rise to quantum fluctuations. This suggests that the vacuum (devoid of any matter) is not really empty but is full of fluctuations and may be considered as a sea of continuously appearing and disappearing particles. Thus, QED has made the vacuum as a truly 'dynamic' entity. The particles that peep out of vacuum cannot be seen or measured directly but they surely leave predictable and measurable effects at quantum level. We call them 'virtual' particles.

Let us look into the interaction between the electron and nucleus inside the atom in the light of QED. This interaction is governed by exchange of field particle 'photon'. During transit, photon may create electron-positron pair and this pair gets annihilated into photon. Remember that all these are 'virtual particles'. This creation and annihilation process continues and a virtual charge cloud is always present in between the electron and nucleus in the atom contrary to what was expected on the basis of quantum mechanics.

We usually picture a particle moving in a line by assuming that it is a point-like object propagating in space. But quantum mechanics (uncertainty principle) suggested us to picture it as a small cloud (wave packet) with undefined boundaries. The newly emerged QED demanded a further change in the picture. According to this, we need to have a dynamic picture of the particle which interacts continuously with its neighbouring environment by emitting and reabsorbing the field particles. Not only this, the particle is also busy in emitting and reabsorbing its own stuff generated in the form of the virtual particles. This gives rise to a completely new picture and effects due the presence of new type of interaction. But this makes the situation terribly complex with computational point of view. Here appears a 'problem of infinity' in the calculations. The QED theory thus suffered with this inherent problem.

As physics cannot deal with infinity, a trick known as 'renormalization' is invented to handle the problem. In this trick, many parameters were assigned 'values' from experimentally known values. The theory however has nothing to say about their origin. QED got solid support, when it explained the puzzling observation of 'Lamb shift', which was observed while investigating the spectral properties of atoms in greater details. The motivation for the physicist Willis Lamb was the availability of newly developed 'microwave technology' after WW-II. During the war-period, scientists worked on many projects to find better ways of destroying the enemy. But after the war, warring nations got exhausted and peace-time prevailed. In the peace-time, mindset changes and physicists turn their attention from 'war-supporting' to 'welfare-supporting' technology. Not only this, they undertake 'curiosity based projects' to create more science that could help them in understanding Nature at deeper level. So, in the peace-time, physicists used to think in a completely different way. Microwave technology was amongst one such technology that played a key-role after World War II. The new awareness of microwave production and sensitive detection techniques led physicists to use microwaves as new tool to study the spectral features of atoms.

Lamb selected the well-studied simplest hydrogen atom for his studies. Hydrogen atom is quite different than other complex atomic systems. There is only one electron in hydrogen atom. So when it is in an excited state, there comes nothing in between the excited electron and the nucleus. The commonly found 'electronic shielding' appears to be absent in hydrogen atom. Each electronic state in hydrogen atom is doubly degenerate i.e. having two components with same energy value. In quantum mechanics, there is nothing that can remove this apparent degeneracy.

Lamb made some finer measurements in the microwave region. He observed a shift that demonstrated the removal of degeneracy. Though the observed shift was very small but was suggestive that the existence of some different kind of operational mechanism other than what was provided by quantum mechanics. He thus demonstrated that the understanding achieved through quantum mechanics of Schrödinger and Dirac failed even in the simplest case of hydrogen. His observation was shocking and puzzling!

Now physicists started looking at the 'Lamb shift' seriously. They looked into newly created QED for resolving the puzzle and finding new inroads in the theoretical understanding of the issue as it was suggesting the presence of fluctuating electromagnetic field in between the electron and the nucleus. This fluctuating field is originating due to continuous appearance and disappearance of short-lived 'virtual' particles. So the 'excited electron' in the degenerate state (having two components, as mentioned above) in the hydrogen atom interacts differently with the nucleus due to the difference in the fluctuating electromagnetic fields in the two cases. Actually, it depends on the nature of the component state in which it is present. Hans Bethe made initial calculations using QED and explained the Lamb shift. This in turn provided a solid proof in support of QED.

After this experimental support, physicists took QED very seriously and started verifying its other predictions. The theory got established and became a new light house to guide future research. We will come on this, later in the book, at appropriate place. At present, let us see how quantum mechanics helped in understanding the properties of materials.

Understanding the properties of matter

The quantum mechanics is employed in order to understand the properties of matter. The physicists believed that these properties must be deeply connected to the electronic structures of matter. The spectroscopic techniques were successfully employed to investigate the electronic structural features of solids. The physicists found the answer to the puzzling question as to why 'neon' and not the 'sodium' is inert. The formation of bonds between atoms in a molecule was understood in great detail. Different types of 'bonding' between different atoms were discovered and justified quantum mechanically.

The x-ray based studies of solids helped in understanding the inter-atomic and intermolecular interactions. The data showed electronic origin of large-scale properties (like thermal, optical, electrical etc.) of matter. This new way of looking at the matter resulted in several technological breakthroughs.

When we look at a 'solid' with quantum eye, we get a very interesting picture. The solids are packed with atoms. We know that the electrons in an atom occupy discrete energy states, but when atoms come together in solid, their electrons occupying the same energy state also come together and their energy states start overlapping. But Pauli's exclusion principle restricts their entry in a single state and so the electrons undergo redistribution. Thus, each energy level gets converted into energy bands to accommodate the identical and indistinguishable electrons that follow Pauli's principle. Two adjacent bands may not be wide enough to cover entire energy range and so gaps appear. The topmost filled electronic band is known as 'valence band' and the empty band as 'conduction band'. The materials were classified on the basis of the energy 'band gap'. For conductors, 'band gap' is zero but for insulators it is very large. Small band gaps give rise to semi-conducting behaviour.

When physicists saw natural material to exhibit various physical properties, they got an idea to manipulate the matter in the hope of meeting some specific technological demands. The 'metals' have free electrons that make them electrically conducting. The 'insulators' have no free electrons and they are tightly bound. There are 'semiconductors', in which the electrons are loosely bound. The 'silicon' and 'germanium' are examples of some well-known semiconductors. It has been noted that the presence of impurities affects the conducting properties to great extent. So, physicists systematically studied the changes in the properties by adding impurities in the solids in a controlled manner.

It has been noticed that when the semiconductors are doped with some impurities, the number of charge carriers may be enhanced and the electrical properties get changed considerably. The nature of the enhanced charge carrier depends upon the nature of impurity. The impurity may add 'electrons' or can create 'vacancy' of electrons. The 'vacancy' of electrons behaves like 'holes' or 'positively charged carriers' in the semiconductor. The electrons remain mobile in the conduction band whereas the 'holes' in the valence band. In order to know the nature of charge carriers responsible for conduction, techniques based on 'Hall Effect', are employed. In this effect a voltage (Hall voltage) generated across a conducting material (say, y-direction), transverse to the direction of electric current (say, x-direction) is measured when there exists a magnetic field in a direction (say, z-direction) which is perpendicular to the electric current. The direction of the Hall voltage indicates the nature of charge carrier.

Soon, new materials were tailored. In the silicon crystal, each silicon atom (having four valence electrons) forms bonds with four neighbouring silicon atoms involving 8 electrons. If one of the silicon is replaced by, say antimony (having five valence electrons), one electron remains unbound. This behaves like free electron and is available for conduction. Thus, by doping silicon or germanium with antimony, we are able to increase the free electrons (n) in them. Opposite happens when silicon is replaced by atom like gallium (having three valence electrons). This creates a deficiency of electrons, which becomes a centre of attraction (trap) for the neighbouring electrons present in the bonds. When an electron from neighbouring silicon atom falls in this trap, a new vacancy is created there. As electron falls in this vacancy, we call it 'hole' (p). Thus, in this case 'hole" is available for conduction.

In this way, 'controlled doping' helped physicists in getting technologically important n- and p- types of semiconductors. A 'p-n' junction is created from these semiconductors as a new solid state electronic component. This development led further to the discovery of 'p-n-p' or 'n-p-n' 'transistor' which soon replaced 'vacuum tube electronics' by 'solid state electronics'. Another technological revolution took birth and we entered in the new era of 'electronics'. Electronics revolutionized everything. It gave us computers, which has become the backbone of all our modern and ultramodern developments.

Up till now, we remained outside the nuclear boundary. We thoroughly studied the electronic structure and observed how physical and chemical properties of matter can emerge. We have seen the discovery of Radioactivity that helped us in knowing some of the structural features of nucleus. Let us now go deeper and see what new clues can be obtained.

Visiting nuclear island

The nucleus was discovered by Rutherford while testing Thomson's atom model by his well-planned alpha particle scattering experiment. He continued his efforts in order to know more about the nucleus using 'α' as probe particles. He thought of breaking the nucleus and thus changing the very nature of elements by bombarding their nuclei by energetic α-particles. His deep insight paved the way for artificial transmutation. It is his first scientific step in realizing the old dream of alchemists to get gold from some other element.

It was known to him that the energy of the naturally emitted α-particles is about 8 MeV. He used them to bombard the molecules of oxygen, carbon dioxide, and nitrogen like gases for his initial experiments. Being massive and energetic, the alpha particles were able to penetrate and collide with the nuclei of the gas molecules. He observed no 'scintillation' with oxygen and carbon dioxide beyond 8 cm but with nitrogen it was observed even at 40 cm. This seemed quite surprising and puzzling. However, it was clear that the 'scintillation' cannot be caused by the same alpha particle. So, Rutherford thought that it could only be possible when the collision produced another particle having long range. But how could this new particle be produced?

The chemical analysis of the gas in the apparatus showed the presence of 'oxygen' which originally contained only nitrogen. Oxygen's presence indicated that a new process is taking place that is changing some of the nitrogen into oxygen. It is like chemical reaction but different than that as the very nature of element is changing here. As the process is taking place at nuclear level, it is called 'nuclear reaction'. In this reaction, alpha particle is absorbed by 'nitrogen' nucleus giving rise to oxygen. In this way, Rutherford quite unexpectedly achieved nuclear transformation and got one element converted into another! A new discovery of artificial transmutation! Interestingly, it is here, a new kind of particle of unknown nature took birth. He then measured the characteristics of this particle by passing it through electric and magnetic fields. He noted that the new particle is a massive (about 1836 times than that of electron) positively charged particle. The magnitude of the charge on the particle is equal to that of electron. This observation prompted Rutherford to think innovatively.

Rutherford intuitively believed that the newly discovered particle must be the basic component of nucleus. He named this particle as 'proton'. Being massive as compared to electron, the major contribution to the atomic mass comes from this particle. He inferred that the presence of electron and proton in equal number makes the atom neutral.

As mentioned earlier, many isotopes were discovered in the meantime. They had different atomic weights but same chemical properties and placed at the same place in periodic table. Keeping this in mind, Rutherford intuitively predicted the presence of neutral 'neutron', a new particle, in the nucleus. However, it was not taken seriously at that time as the common sense started guiding. The beta emission, discovery of electron and proton were available as better guides at that time. So, for nuclear structure, it was obvious to think electron and proton as basic components. Soon, 'proton-electron model' of nucleus emerged. This model got initial support from the radioactive emission of beta particles (i.e. electrons). The logical thinking helped in predicting some of the basic properties of nuclei like magnetic moment and spin. But nothing came out as per expectations. Soon, it was clear to the physicists that electron could not be a constituent of nucleus. Their confidence was built up on solid experimental grounds. So, the physicists started taking Rutherford's prediction about the presence of 'neutrons' in the nucleus seriously. The story of the discovery of neutron is very interesting.

While studying the disintegration of the Beryllium nuclei by α-particles (emitting out from radioactive polonium), physicists W.G. Bothe and H. Becker observed the emission of highly penetrating mysterious radiation. Magnetic deflection experiment failed to give any information about the nature of the particles constituting these radiations. So, they speculated them to be made of 'gamma ray photons'. Then, Frédéric Joliot and Irène Curie used this mysterious radiation to produce artificial transmutation (i.e. to transform one element to another). Further, when they performed collision experiments between the particle (speculated gamma ray photon) and those fixed in the target used in the form of hydrogenous material like paraffin/ water/ paper/ cellophane, they noted that the production of the protons of energy 5 MeV having range of about 40 cm. in air. Their calculations showed that to produce such a proton, the energy of the speculated γ-ray photon constituting mysterious radiation should be about 50 MeV. But this value was found to be far higher than the actual measurements of the speculated γ-ray photons, performed using a calorimeter (an apparatus that measures the heat produced during any reactions or process), which is only about 7 MeV. So, the problem was not getting resolved. It was here that James Chadwick recalled Rutherford's ignored neutron hypothesis. He thought that maybe the particles of mysterious radiations are neutrons. He looked at the proton's energy obtained from the collisions using different targets like paraffin, nitrogen, helium, carbon, nitrogen and oxygen and found a theoretical inconsistency. His estimation of energy of the particle of the mysterious radiation has shown its dependence on the nature of target material. Logically, this cannot be true unless the law of conservation of energy gets failed. Having strong faith in the validity of conservation laws, he planned another experiment to know the exact nature of the particles. He was well aware of the fact that γ-rays are shielded by lead. So, in this experiment, he allowed the mysterious rays to pass through a thick lead wall and observed that it is not in position to shield these rays. He further noted that there was also no any significant change in the penetration power of the mysterious rays, whether lead is used or not. It is as if lead is transparent to these radiations. After this rational thinking, there remained no doubt in his mind that the mysterious radiations are not made of 'γ-ray photons' but of 'neutrons'. So, he confidently announced the discovery of 'neutron'. In this way, 'neutron' was discovered quite intelligently by Chadwick as a new fundamental particle of matter.

After the discovery of neutron, the 'proton-neutron' model of nucleus was proposed. Interestingly, but unbelievably the positively charged 'protons' along with their companion neutral 'neutrons' confined in a very small region. This is the region where large repulsive Coulombian forces dominate. How can a stable nucleus be formed in the presence of these forces? But existence of stable nucleus is a reality. So the question arose why didn't the nucleus split apart? What held them together? Scientists of those days were really puzzled. However, it appeared clear that something must exist in the nuclear space which helped in gluing the protons.

Discovery of nuclear strong force

Hideki Yukawa got interested in the problem and developed a theory by hypothesizing the existence of strong nuclear force. He envisaged a particle 'meson' whose exchange between the neighbouring particles produces this force. The influence of the anticipated force should extend only in the nuclear dimensions (about 2 x 10^{-15} m) enabling nuclear particles to be confined within nucleus. So, it must be a 'short range attractive force'. This force should overpower the Coulombian (electromagnetic) repulsive force inside the nuclei. It is clear that without such force, nucleus would disintegrate. With increasing size of nucleus, the nuclear force starts decreasing and the Coulombian force starts increasing. There should be a tug of war between them. The crowded nucleus exhibit radioactivity and continue decaying till stability is achieved.

In physics, force between the interacting entities is produced by the exchange of a force carrier particle. The short-range of the Yukawa's force needed massive particle (much heavier than the electron) 'meson', the particle to be exchanged. It appeared unbelievable at first sight, but the process had its operational justification through Heisenberg's uncertainty principle.

Neutrons and protons in 'isotopic space'

The physicists discovered certain special type of nuclei called 'mirror nuclei'. In these nuclei, the sum of neutrons and protons remains the same but the number of neutron and proton are interchanged. The binding energy remains unaffected by this interchange. Further, the members of the pair exhibit identical set of energy levels. The spin of these nuclei also remains the same. This suggests that the nuclear force responsible for the nuclear binding is 'charge-independent' and so the neutron and proton might be treated as 'two states of a single particle'. This is named 'nucleon'. To give a theoretical base to this idea, Heisenberg proposed a new space of abstract nature called the 'isotopic space' in which the two particles are present with 'isotopic spin' states as either 'up' or 'down'. The nuclear force being 'charge independent', remains the same between 'two protons' or 'two neutrons' or between 'a neutron and a proton'.

Discovery of fourth fundamental force

As mentioned earlier, the beta decay gave a hint of the presence of electrons in the nucleus. Keeping this in mind, physicists expected much higher value of magnetic moment. But the observed value of 'magnetic moment' was much smaller. This clearly indicated that the existence of free electrons in the nucleus was not possible. But by this, the fact of beta particle's emission remained challenging and incomprehensible. So, physicists started thinking innovatively. They suggested that the beta particle was emitted from the nucleus by some other process and took birth at the time of emission. Fermi later developed a theory. Soon we will come on this. This time, let us concentrate on some important observations related to beta emission. The experiments showed that the sum total of the energy of the 'beta particle' and the 'product nucleus' decay was less than that of the decaying nucleus, as if the law of conservation energy was not holding good there. But, it was unbelievable. Where was the energy going after all? Could a particle getting emitted during the process exist there? Could this particle, carrying the unaccounted energy away, remain unnoticed?

It was the time, when physicists discovered many empirical facts of Nature and enunciated them in the form of conservation laws. These facts were known from the observation of symmetries existing in Nature. Under symmetries, some specific properties of the system remained preserved. Physicists observed 'space' to be 'homogeneous and isotropic'. The mathematical understanding of these symmetries emerged respectively as conservation of linear and angular momenta. The 'isotropy of time' led the emergence of law of conservation of energy. All these laws were firmly established without any failure.

Wolfgang Pauli was the strong believer of conservation laws. So, he predicted confidently that the puzzling unaccounted energy during beta decay should be associated by the the simultaneous emission of one more particle. Pauli called this new hypothetical particle as 'little neutron' but Enrico Fermi gave it the name 'neutrino'. It carries no charge and was initially believed to be mass-less. However, later it is found to possess some mass.

Fermi developed a theory for beta decay and showed that this process is governed by a new type of short range 'weak nuclear interaction'. It is 'fourth' type of fundamental interaction of Nature. This interaction causes a nucleon to change its state. Two types of decays are possible. In one decay process, 'neutron' changes into 'proton' producing 'electron' and in the other process 'proton' changes into 'neutron' producing 'positron'. They are called 'beta negative' (β^-)' and 'beta positive' (β^+) processes. As predicted, the 'neutrino' accompanies 'beta' during both the types of decays. If neutrino had not been included in the emitted products, the spin would not have remained conserved. So, inclusion of neutrino not only saved the energy conservation law but also the spin angular momentum conservation law.

We will come on 'neutrino' later in this book. This time, let us go back in the nuclear world where physicists were busy in bombarding the nuclei by 'alpha particles' and also by newly discovered 'neutrons' in order to learn more about nucleus and nuclear properties. They started with the curiosity based question 'can there be atoms beyond atomic number 92?' Can artificial atoms with high atomic numbers be created? Study of some heavy radioactive atoms provided a clue to understand the mechanism of transformation of one kind of matter into another. This has made alchemist's dream a reality!

On the way of creating new elements

Irène Curie and Frédéric Joliot while bombarding an aluminum target with alpha-particles noticed that the aluminum continued to radiate even after they had stopped the alpha-particle bombardment. In this way accidently, they discovered 'artificial radioactivity'.

Success of the alpha particle based collision experiments motivated physicists to use some other particles as probe. As alpha particle and the nucleus of the target atom are positive, so they naturally repel each other. In order to overcome this, high speed particles are required. Fermi decided and tried to produce artificial radioactivity by bombarding the elements with neutrons. Neutrons are ideal as they are able to penetrate even the heavier nuclei without being repelled. Fermi tried by using the neutrons of varying speeds. For changing the speed of neutrons, he passed them through 'paraffin', whose molecules acted as 'retarders'. He bombarded a series of elements by neutrons and discovered many new radioactive elements (radioisotopes). The total number of the elements has now reached over 115, including the natural ones. Further, while working with slow neutrons, he found quite accidently the breaking (fission) of uranium nucleus into approximately two halves. Let us learn something more about nuclear fission.

Nuclear Fission – Twentieth century energy source

In this process of fission, heavy nuclei brake but surprisingly, a part of the nuclear mass gets converted into energy. Calculations indicated that this is exactly the amount that is expected from Einstein's mass-energy formula. The discovery was made during the period of war and so it attracted the attention of 'power seekers politicians'. 'Manhattan Project' in US was initiated with the purpose of war. Based on the concept, an atom bomb was successfully built and tested. The energy produced by 1.0 g of uranium is equivalent to that produced by 20000 tonnes of TNT! Later the bomb was used and the World War II ended... The use of atom bomb against humanity brought an ugly face of science before society. The world got horrified and social pressure started building up. So, physicists diverted their attention after the war and began to think of the peaceful applications of nuclear research. The atomic reactors were soon developed to stop the uncontrolled way of production of energy through atom bomb. They optimistically looked at it as a new source of energy. While working with neutron beams, they also discovered some 'radioactive nuclei' which could be used as 'radio tracers'. The radio tracers were found quite useful as diagnostic tools in solving many of the medical and agricultural problems. . The nuclear physics thus extended its helping hand in solving the problems of society.

Let us go back at the theoretical developments which made predictions and opened new dimensions to go for deeper understanding of matter and its constitution. It was the time when three new particles, positron (i.e. antielectron), meson and neutrino were predicted theoretically.

Mysterious particle world

The predictions of new types of particles mentioned above were having solid theoretical grounds but their experimental confirmation seemed to be a difficult task. As we have seen, the neutrino, being a very weakly interacting particle, posed a greater challenge. However for discovering other particles, high energy collisions and sensitive detectors were needed. But the technological advancements, in those days, were too meager to produce highly energetic particle beams, required to produce desired effects through energy-mass conversions, in the laboratories. Radioactivity and the cosmic rays were the only known natural sources for getting energetic particles. The alpha particles obtained from radioactive nuclei had earlier been tried by Rutherford and other physicists. But the energy of the particles from these natural resources was not sufficient to test the predictions. So, the physicists looked optimistically at cosmic rays. These rays contain highly energetic protons and likelihood of their interaction with air particles was not small. The chances of observing the desired collision events are bright when highly energetic protons enter the earth's atmosphere and collide with air particles. In order to record such events, the earlier invention of 'cloud chamber' by C.R.T. Wilson was found to be of great value. The 'cloud chamber' operates on the simple physics of cloud formation. In this chamber, an ionizing particle leaves a trail of water droplets, which can be photographed.

The physicists build 'cosmic-ray observatories' on mountains at high altitudes where the probability of natural occurrence of interesting collisions is high. Now, the cosmic ray observatories have become the new venue of physicists. The hunt for the predicted particles began in cosmic laboratories by detectors like cloud chambers. The cloud chamber photographs may be analyzed in order to know the kind of particle that passed through, its life-time, energy and the outcome of its interaction with the atmospheric particles. By placing the detector in magnetic fields, one can also know with confidence the particles' momentum and the charge.

Cosmic laboratory

While working on cosmic rays, Carl Anderson recorded an event in a 'cloud chamber' in which he observed a track of electron-like particle but with positive charge. It was nothing but 'positron', 'anti-particle' of electron. Thus, the Dirac's theoretical prediction was verified by this discovery. The existence of predicted 'antimatter' has become a new reality now! This brought a paradigm shift in the very approach of looking at the universe.

Now scientists hoped that the cosmic ray studies could give them some more clues to uncover the secrets of Nature. But for this, they were to keep their eyes wide open and wait for the events to naturally occur. Carl Anderson continued and discovered a 'meson' which had approximately the same mass as predicted by Yukawa. But this 'meson' was found to interact very weakly with the nucleus, contrary to what was expected for the Yukawa's predicted meson. Yukawa's meson must interact very strongly with the nuclear matter. So, finding it different in behaviour, it was named as mu-meson or 'muon'. It behaved just like very heavy electron (about 210 times heavier than electron) but with very short-life and was found to decay into electron. Though this newly discovered particle was not Yukawa's meson but it was certainly a discovery that signaled the existence of structural complexity of the matter. Yukawa's meson was discovered later by Physicist Cecil Frank Powell and his colleagues in the cosmic laboratory, 12 years after its prediction. It was named 'pion'. Few more particles were discovered during the study of cosmic rays making the picture hazy and complicated. Let us look into some of the important discoveries.

Physicists G. D. Rochester and Clifford Charles Butler, while studying events associated with cosmic rays, noticed tracks in their cloud chamber. These could only be explained by the decay of a neutral particle with a mass about 1000 times greater than that of the electron. It was a new kind of meson, named 'kaon'.

The 'kaons' were found to exhibit puzzling behaviour. It was noticed that some of them decay into two 'pions' while the remaining into three pions. Naturally, physicists thought them to be of two different types and called them 'tau' and 'theta' particles respectively. But when masses and lifetimes of the particles were measured accurately, it appeared that they were not different particles. But then the question arose, how the same particle could decay in two different ways giving different number of pions. For this to be allowed, the law of conservation of parity (left-right symmetry) needs to be broken. Keeping this in mind, physicists looked at the strange behaviour of this particle with respect to this 'parity'.

For the physicists, there was no difference between the 'world' and its 'mirror image'. They were of the opinion that Nature cannot distinguish between left and right and so left-right symmetry must be preserved. Technically, we call this as law of conservation of parity. It was a cherished law up till now. No any event had been reported in the literature that showed the failure of this law. However, tau-theta puzzle raised the doubt. If the parity is to remain conserved then the 'tau' and 'theta' need to be two different particles. And if they represent the same particle, then, we need to overthrow this law. The situation was quite confusing.

Physicists Lee and Yang decided to remove the confusion. They carefully reviewed the existing data and found plenty of evidences that validate the law. But they were surprised to note that none of the evidence was related to the events governed by weak interactions. The kaonic decay is governed by weak interaction, so they intuitively guessed that the 'tau' and 'theta' should be the same particle and the parity conservation law should be violated in this case. Confident Yang and Lee didn't stop here but hypothesized that not only the kaons but all other particles, whose decay is governed by weak interaction, do not follow the law of parity conservation. It was against the conventional belief. But it was surely a bold proposal and a great step forward. It not only helped in resolving the puzzle but showed directions in which a whole new area of activity may be initiated. Lee and Yang suggested several experiments to determine the left-right symmetry during the decay.

Inspired by Lee and Yang, Madame Chien-Shiung Wu planned an experiment to test the hypothesis. In her experiment she placed ultra-cooled beta-emitting nuclei in a magnetic field and observed anisotropic emission of beta decay. She noticed that the emitted beta particles were preferentially emitted in the direction opposite to that of the aligned angular momentum of the nuclei. In this way, she discovered parity violation and demonstrated the hypothesis of Lee and Yang to be correct.

In spite of these revolutionary developments, the belief of physicists in symmetry did not shake. Instead, scientists started thinking about more perfect symmetry to lie at deeper level. They thought that combined conservation of C and P i.e. CP symmetry must hold.

The changes in symmetry properties in which some property of the quantum object (space, time or charge) is reflected or reversed can be understood by an analogy of a "mirror". A real mirror reflection provides a concrete example of this because mirror reflection reverses the space direction perpendicular to the plane of the mirror. As a consequence, the mirror image of a right-handed glove is a left-handed glove. This is in effect a parity transformation (although a true P transformation should reverse all three spatial axes instead of only one).

After Wu's experiment, it becomes possible to distinguish between the object and its mirror-image. The electron is real but not its mirror image. In other words, beta (β^-) and all the 'particles' are left handed i.e. their direction of motion is opposite to that of their spin direction. The image of beta (β^-) in which both are parallel is not found in Nature. As a result, the world we live in is distinguishable from its mirror image.

If the mirror reversed not only the spatial direction but also changed matter to antimatter, then the experiment performed in front of the mirror would look like the mirror-image of Wu's experiment in which beta (β^-) emitter is replaced by beta (β^+) emitter. This time, the beta (β^+) particles would prefer opposite direction for its emission as observed in original Wu's experiment. The separate violations of P symmetry (i.e. change of handedness from left to right) and C symmetry (i.e. change of particle to anti-particle) cancel each other's effects to preserve CP symmetry. It may be remembered that each particle has its corresponding anti-particle. The particle is assigned quantum number '1' while '-1' is assigned to anti-particle. The total quantum number corresponding to particles and anti-particles is conserved during any nuclear event. To understand it, let us recall the example of beta (β^-) decay in which anti-neutrino must be emitted along with proton and electron (particles) in order to satisfy required conservation law. Here, we can also notice one more interesting point. Before decay, there was only one entity governed by strong interaction (giving corresponding quantum number '1') and no entity governed by weak interaction (giving corresponding quantum number 'zero). But after decay, we have three entities, out of which one is a governed by strong interaction (giving corresponding quantum number '1') and the two by weak interaction, in which one is particle and the other is anti-particle (giving corresponding quantum number 'zero'). Thus, the particles are also conserved on the basis of the way they interact. Later, we will explore this conservation law at much deeper level. This time, let us have few words on CPT symmetry.

CPT symmetry

Physicists believe that no asymmetries will be found after reversing charge, space, and time. So, they expected Nature to possess minimum CPT symmetry. Therefore, CP symmetry implies the existence of T-symmetry (or time reversal invariance) in Nature. However it doesn't appeal to our common sense, which is based on our daily life experiences. Our common sense is built on the preferred direction of time arrow. We know how to differentiate between the forward or backward moving times. But at quantum level, there are no ways to distinguish. No physical law differentiates between forward and backward directions of time. The everyday experience of "arrow of time" does not work here. Both directions are equally preferred and probable. That's why the 'combined CP' was believed to be a 'valid' symmetry of the Universe. But soon the scenario changed. In 1964, J.H. Christenson, J.W. Cronin, V.L. Fitch and R. Turlay gave an evidence of violation of CP symmetry while experimenting with neutral kaons. Actually, physicists discovered two types of kaons, distinguishable on the basis of their life. They have been termed as 'short' and 'long' lived kaons. The long-lived neutral kaon has been found to decay into two pions, but this was against what was expected on the basis of CP symmetry. If CP were a natural symmetry, it could only decay to three pions, not two. If CPT symmetry is to be preserved, the CP violation must be compensated by a violation of time reversal invariance.

Indeed later experiments on neutral kaons have shown that the decay probabilities are really different in forward and reverse directions. This brought a turning point in the history of physics as the T-violations are connected with the deep mystery of imbalance between matter and antimatter found in the universe (at the time of birth of the universe both are equal). Only T-violation could answer the question as to why do we have abundance of 'matter' (and, not anti-matter) in the universe today.

Let us take a pause here and go back to see what experimental physicists have done in the meantime to expand the particle-world.

Discovery of neutrino!

The 'neutrino' eluded for quite some years. It was predicted while explaining beta decay. It was taking time because it interacts very weakly with matter. It would take 10^{19} m (300 light years, which is the distance travelled by light in 300 years) long column of water to absorb a single neutrino. Therefore we need many neutrinos and a very large detector. During beta (β^-) decay, neutron transforms into proton and an anti-neutrino is produced. Its inverse is also probable in which proton absorbs antineutrino and gets transformed into neutron by producing anti-electron i.e. positron. Similarly during beta (β^+) decay, proton decays into a neutron and neutrino is produced. Its inverse is also possible in which neutron absorbs neutrino and gets converted into proton by producing electron. This forms the basis for the design of experiment that can help in detecting the footprint of neutrino. But huge particle detectors of special types were required to record such rare events. Physicists were trying to get rid of technological hurdles. The hope got further enhanced when the physicists could locate the places where neutrinos can be found in abundance. The core of stars is the most favourite natural locations. But the 'nuclear test and reactor sites' are among some accessible terrestrial locations for getting antineutrino flux.

Further, it is known that when antineutrino interacts with a proton, neutron is produced along with positron during inverse decay process. If the appropriate detector is chosen, the 'positron' may get annihilated with the 'electron' present in the detector giving rise to two photons moving in opposite directions (in accordance of conservation laws). The simultaneous emission of these photons may be known by using scintillating material in the detector. Actually, scintillating material gives visible flashes, which can be detected by photomultipliers (extremely sensitive light detectors). Logically water (having abundance of protons needed to interact with antineutrinos) mixed with some scintillating material (to convert gamma ray photons into flushes of light in visible range) may be chosen in the detector. But can this evidence be sufficient and present a confirmative proof? No, it cannot be sufficient. We need to detect the 'leftover' neutron too. 'Cadmium' may be used for the purpose as it is well-known 'neutron absorber'. When cadmium absorbs neutron, it emits gamma ray photon which may again be detected by the photomultiplier. Of course after a short delay, as the theory suggests, the neutron absorption process to occur after completion of positron-electron annihilation process. So, the detection of these three photons should provide the proof of the footprint of neutrino. This is all that came in the mind of Frederick

Reines and Clyde L. Cowan, Jr. Now, they were ready and started putting their efforts in order to realize their idea. They selected a suitable nuclear test and reactor sites to be used as neutrino source and installed a huge detector. It had two tanks with 200 liters of water containing 40 kg cadmium chloride. They employed innovative detection technique in which the water tanks were sandwiched between three scintillator layers which contained photomultipliers. They finally succeeded in recording sufficient events and discovered this eluding neutrino. It was a great discovery!

Soon after Reins and Cowen's discovery, efforts to detect solar neutrino (emission of neutrinos from the sun) began. For this a new technique is followed. This is based on the interaction of neutrino with chlorine. We know that the nucleus of chlorine contains 17 protons and 18 neutrons. When neutrino interacts with chlorine, it gets absorbed by one of the neutrons present there and converts it into proton. This transforms 'chlorine' into radioactive 'argon'. The detection of argon gives a proof of neutrino passed through detector. The probability, however, is so small that out of 10^{30} chlorine atoms, only 10 chlorine nuclei interact producing 10 argon atoms in one month! Though the probability is extremely low, but is non-zero and so can be recorded. This feat is achieved by Raymond Davis and John N. Bahcall. This is famous as 'Homestake or Davis experiment' in the literature. Several other innovative techniques were discovered and 'neutrino telescopes' and 'neutrino observatories' were set up in later years.

Neutrino's discovery created new interest and a host of activities began around this. Soon the neutrino became so important that physicists looked at it as the most 'precious key' to unlock the secrets of the Nature. We will talk about the puzzling results obtained while measuring the solar neutrino flux, later at appropriate place. At present, let us see the creation of bizarre scene that emerged during the particle-collisions experiments both in cosmic and man-made laboratories. In these experiments, the energy of the colliding particles gets converted into mass (according to Einstein's mass-energy relation) and produces a pair of particle and anti-particle. But, when particle meets its anti-particle, an equivalent amount of energy is produced which may create entirely new type of particles.

Cosmic dance

In cosmic laboratory, sometimes energy appears as mass and sometimes the mass as energy. This bizarre scene is created through an interplay of 'quantum mechanics' and 'Einstein's relativity'. Soon, the Nature is caught performing a cosmic dance! It mesmerized the physics community.

The results coming from the cosmic laboratory were quite interesting and making physicists very curious. Physicists were interested in getting data at high speed to understand the matter and the interactions but the wishful high energy collision events in cosmic laboratory were too rare and infrequent. Thus, they had to wait for long and depend heavily on chance and luck. This motivated them to create facilities in the laboratories to produce required highly energetic particles.

Collision study in labs

Physicists have undertaken a programme to invent particle accelerators. For the development of such machines, the knowledge gained from the behavioural studies of charged particles in presence of electric and magnetic fields is used. They successfully developed many machines like linear accelerator, cyclotron, synchrotron etc. When the high-energetic particle beams are produced in the laboratories, physicists have started planning and performing 'collision experiments' at different desired energies.

In order to record collision events, physicists turned their attention on the development of sensitive detectors. They recalled the 'emulsion techniques' used in ordinary photography. Photo sensitive, silver halide grains dispersed in gelatin forms what is known as 'emulsion'. The gelatin provided a 'three dimensional network' which serves to locate the small grain of the halide and to prevent them migrating during development and fixation of the image. The Emulsion technique was first used by Becquerel while studying radioactivity and then it was greatly improved after the development of electron-sensitive emulsions and the availability of high-resolution microscopes.

The emulsion technique helped in developing a new type of particle detector and preferred over widely used cloud chamber technique because of its enhanced sensitivity. When the charged particles or electromagnetic radiation passes through an emulsion detector, it leaves a track. The properties of the track depend on the charge, mass and speed of the particle. In the developed photographic plate, a chain of black grains along the trail of the particle is produced. The tracks are observed by microscope and carefully analyzed. Many new types of particles were detected using this technique.

After this emulsion detector, 'bubble chamber' was developed. The bubble chamber is based on the simple physics of bubble formation. It is filled with liquid hydrogen which is quite suitable when target is to be used as proton. Say for example, a physicist interested in finding the outcome of an interaction between 'antiproton and proton' or in between 'pion and proton', needs to have antiproton or pion beam and a bubble chamber. In an experiment, when a beam of antiproton is incident towards bubble chamber, antiproton interacts with a proton waiting there. After collision both of them get annihilated. The energy produced is enough to create number of particles of lighter mass and to give them enough kinetic energy. But the creation of the particles is governed by certain conservation laws. That's why some reactions otherwise expected to occur were never observed. For example the annihilation of electron and positron produces two gamma ray photons but never a single photon (as we have seen earlier during the description of neutrino detection). The neutron decays into proton and electron but never without an anti-neutrino. The neutral pion decays producing two gamma ray photons but never single photon.

During the experiments, one puzzling result was obtained. It was about the decay products of muon. The decay of positively charged muon gave positron, neutrino and antineutrino but never produced the theoretically expected gamma ray photon. The same was with the decay of negatively charged muon. The results were difficult to understand on the basis of knowledge gained so far and appeared quite puzzling.

New flavour of Neutrino

Jack Steinberger was a student of Enrico Fermi and on his advice got interested in deeper study of weak interaction. He invited Leon M. Lederman and Melvin Schwartz to join the project. They looked into the then puzzling problem of 'muon-decay'. For this they built a large 'spark chamber' and got a beam of poins by directing intense proton beam on beryllium target. During collision, pi-mesons were produced. The pi-mesons decayed and gave rise to collimated beam of muons and neutrinos. A steel shield of 13.0 m thickness was used to stop all particles except the neutrinos. The pi-mesons interacting through the strong force were stopped early, while the muons, interacting mainly through the electromagnetic force, penetrated much deeper. These muons got decayed and produced neutrinos. Interestingly these neutrinos after interaction produced only muons but no electrons. Had there been equal number of muons and electrons produced, there would have remained no doubt for it to be the same type of neutrino as that predicted and detected earlier. But the production of only muons clearly indicated that the neutrino detected in this experiment is different than that discovered earlier. This implied further that the neutrinos have inherent 'birth marks' and are identified accordingly. The 'neutrino' detected by Reins and Coven earlier was associated with electron and should now be called as 'electron neutrino' and not only as 'neutrino' keeping in mind its birth mark. Similarly the neutrino discovered in this experiment is associated with muon and be called muon-neutrino. In this way, we get 'electron and electron neutrino' and 'muon and muon neutrino' as two distinct families maintaining their identity. The particles of these families are 'spin-half particles' and are not governed by strong nuclear force. They have been given a generalized name 'lepton'. Further, it has been noted that during any interaction, total lepton number ('1' for lepton and '-1' for anti-lepton) of each family remains conserved independently. This implies that we got two 'families' in the lepton category of particles, each one having two members. Later, we will see one more family with two more members, taon and tau-neutrino, joining the lepton category.

Particles and their life time

Many studies showed that particles decay after certain life. Some of them show higher and some extremely small average life. The proton, electron, neutrino and photon along with their respective antiparticles are stable. The rest of the particles are unstable and are characterized by the range of their lifetimes. There are three categories, long-lived, short-lived and infinitely short-lived. The first category covers a wide range extending from 10^3s to 10^{10}s. The second category falls in the range around 10^{-16}s. The third called resonances are found to have lifetime around 10^{-23}s. The neutrino and photon have infinite life.

It should be remembered that in the particle world, it is impossible to predict the actual lifetime. We can only talk of probability of decay. Speaking about lifetime doesn't mean the life of individual particle. It is the average property associated with the members of community. For example, the temperature of the gas doesn't mean the temperature of the individual molecules. Further, it should also be made clear that the decay of the elementary particles must not be understood in literary sense. It should also be remembered that the decay products are not actually present in the decaying particles as constituents. So, the decay products never form the structure of the particle.

Particle laboratories started yielding

With growing interest, many particle physics labs were set up in the world. One of the major international laboratories is CERN (European Council for Nuclear Research), where the Large Hadron Collider (LHC) in which two highly energetic proton beams collide head-on is installed. LHC is a large scale worldwide scientific cooperation project. In August, 2013, 'bigbang-2' experiment has successfully been performed here. A lot of data have been collected and are being in the process of interpretation. One result is out which made much talked Higgs boson a reality. Some other important labs are Brookhaven National Laboratory, Lawrence Berkeley Laboratory and Fermilab of US, Budker Institute of Nuclear Physics in Russia and DESY (*Deutsches Elektronen*-Synchrotron) in Germany.

In the 'particle physics laboratories', physicists performed many high-energy collision experiments and discovered charged and neutral pions, kaons, zie, lamda and sigma like particles. At number of occasions, the products have more mass than the initial colliding particles. This suggests that the kinetic energy is getting converted into mass in accordance with the theory of relativity. But the particles are not created randomly. The initial particles involved in the conversion process are governed by the conservation laws. At occasions, some particles, whose production is not governed by the existing conservation laws, are produced.

The 'kaon' and 'sigma' are such particles that are always produced in pair during 'pion-proton interaction'. The process is governed by strong interaction. Production of the particles in pair, without fail, gave hint about the presence of some inherent property, not known till then, hidden in them. Physicists noticed that the particles decayed unexpectedly slowly and exhibited very large lifetime (of the order of 10^{-10} s). However, their production in pion-proton reactions proceeds much faster (in about 10^{-23} s). Keeping in mind their strange behavior, Abraham Pais introduced a new property 'strangeness (S)' to be associated with them. Further, he turned his attention on the production of the particles in the form of pair. As the interacting particles do not possess this strangeness, the total sum of strangeness associated with the particles of the pair must be zero. This indicated the quantum nature of this property that must remain conserved during this interaction. In this way a new law of 'conservation of strangeness' was discovered. This law is followed by the processes governed by strong interaction. Further kaons slowly decay via weak interaction into pions with zero strangeness; we infer that the law of strangeness fails during weak decay or interaction.

The discovery of hadrons with the internal quantum number 'strangeness' marks the beginning of a new era in 'particle physics'. The collision experiments have started pouring many new results. Observation of the 'energy-mass inter-conversion' has become a regular feature in the laboratories.

It is now not difficult to imagine that by increasing kinetic energy, one can hope to observe the processes in which the number and types of particles may vary. Thus a proton on colliding with another proton may produce (1) three protons and an anti-proton or (2) zie, positive kaon and neutral kaon, or (3) neutral lamda, positive kaon and positive pion, or (4) a proton and positive sigma along with neutral kaon, or (5) a proton and positive kaon along with neutral lambda, or (6) a proton and neutron along with neutral pion. The possibilities are endless. We can even imagine that the two protons with infinite energy can create the whole universe!

Following the line of Rutherford, scientists started other 'quantum objects' to probe the structural features of the constituents of nucleus at deeper level. After developing facilities for getting high energetic electron beam, a new series of scattering experiments have been undertaken by physicists.

The electron scattering experiments had distinct advantage over other experiments because the electrons do not interact with the nucleus through 'strong' nuclear interaction. They interact primarily through well-understood coulombian interaction. The electrons may, however, interact with nucleus through 'weak' nuclear interaction but it is negligibly small during the scattering.

Nucleons – The fuzzy balls!

Electron scattering experiments gave detailed information about the charge distribution within the nuclear volume. The experiments are simple. In concept, they are similar to Rutherford alpha particle scattering experiment. It involves the shooting of the high-energy electrons at thin target of material under study and observing the probability of various angular deflections. Experiments showed that the proton or neutron is not just a uniform 'fuzzy ball'. There are some areas inside the ball that are less dense than its other areas, which establishes that the proton may have some internal structure. Three distinct areas were found in the nucleons. Richard Feynman proposed 'parton model' to explain the results. 'Parton' was later recognized as 'quark'. This suggested that the nuclear particles like protons or neutrons are 'composite' particles and are not truly 'elementary'. This observation led to the development of 'quark theory' in the following years. We will come on 'quark' soon.

Efforts to understand particle world

Soon, physicists started witnessing the arrival of a flood of particles during the studies of high-energy particle collision experiments. Appearance of large number of particles in the 'scene' was a cause of worry. After all, how many particles may truly be called 'elementary'? Now understanding their behaviour was a great challenge before scientists. Can we know few basic building blocks which can be used to understand the diverse world of particles? Can the particles be arranged in few categories for ease of understanding? These were some of the questions before the then physicists.

Let us analyze and rationalize the data collected so far in order to find some threads which can finally be woven to get a simplified picture.

In search of classification basis

The quantum objects are characterized by their inherent 'spin'. But they cannot have any arbitrary value of spin. Whatever may be the nature of quantum object, it may either possess odd or even multiple of half integral unit of spin angular momentum. Any other value is not permitted by Nature. This inherent property of the elementary particles suggests that they may statistically be dealt only by two different types of statistics and they are 'Fermi Dirac (FD)' and 'Bose Einstein (BE)' statistics. The particles following FD statistics are known as 'fermions' and those following BE statistics are 'bosons'. So, all the particles may be grouped under two categories. But it is general and broad classification. For elementary particles, we require some different classification.

Let us look into some other properties of fermions and bosons. From the data, we notice that the particles have variable mass, but they fall into few groups. Particles having mass 'in between that of proton and electron' are termed as 'mesons'. But with the increasing number of mesons, there arose a confusion. So, the physicists thought of changing the basis of major classification from 'mass' to the nature of their 'interaction'. Four types of fundamental interactions have so far been discovered. They are 'gravitational', 'electromagnetic', 'nuclear strong' and 'nuclear weak' interactions. In the particle world, we encounter all but gravitational interaction at low-energy scale (at high energy, gravitational effects may not be negligible because of dominant relativistic effects). Keeping in mind the interactions, the particles governed by strong interaction have been categorized as 'hadrons'. They have been observed to fall in two categories on the basis of mass criterion and need sub-classification. So, the hadrons have further been sub-classified as 'baryons' and 'mesons'. The baryons include 'nucleons' (the proton and neutron) and 'hyperons' (particles heavier than nucleons). It may be interesting to note that all mesons behave like bosons whereas hyperons behave like fermions. Now look at the remaining types of particles. Some of them are governed by 'weak interaction' and classified as 'leptons'. Interestingly, all leptons behave like fermions. Finally, we remain with only those particles which are involved in the fundamental interactions. They have been classified as 'field bosons' and are also known as 'force carriers'. These particles are being exchanged between the particles during interaction.

Now, it is clear that the matter can be understood in terms of 'leptons' and 'hadrons'. Though the number of stable leptons and hadrons is limited but the hadrons are much larger in number. So, a better understanding of hadrons is required.

Discovering hadron patterns

Following an innovative approach, Murray Gell-Mann and Yuval Ne'man tried to observe the underlying symmetries in the hadrons. They made 'charge versus strangeness plots' for baryons and mesons. To their surprise, they got some fascinating 'hexagonal' and 'triangular' symmetrical patterns. Inspired by earlier historical development of the formation of few groups of chemical elements in periodic table, they started moving forward and building their ideas confidently. Murray Gell-Mann, while arranging baryons, noticed that a particle is missing to get a 'triangular pattern'. But his strong faith in symmetry inspired him to predict the existence of a particle 'omega' with appropriate but unusual properties that was required to complete the pattern. His prediction guided experimentalist Nicholas Samios, who succeeded in discovering it. Thus, the faith in symmetry in developing the understanding of the Nature got strengthened.

Above mentioned events in the particle world reminded of the well-known periodic table in which the chemical elements were arranged in few groups on the basis of atomic weight. But, they were later found to be related to the internal structure of atom. Can a similar 'reality' exist in the particle-world too? Can all the mesons and baryons be made of some more fundamental building blocks? How to penetrate deeper in the nuclear matter? With these questions in mind, physicists started looking into the finer structural details.

Quarks in the way

The initial idea came from the electron scattering results which showed nucleons to possess composite structures. This result motivated physicists to think in this line. All particles governed by strong interaction may possess nucleon like structures. Their structures are expressible in terms of some more fundamental particles 'quarks'.

So, an innovative approach was suggested to look at the hadron world of particles with newly emerged concept of 'quark'. Soon a 'quark model' was proposed to understand the particles discovered so far and governed by strong interaction. The quarks are fermions which, have been hypothesized to possess fractional electric charge, of value either '+2/3' or '-1/3' of the electronic charge. Initially only three quarks, 'up', 'down' and 'strange', were thought to be sufficient to deal with them. According to the model, proton is composed of two 'up' quarks and one 'down' quark, whereas a neutron is made of two 'down' quarks and one 'up' quark. The kaons like particles showing strange behaviour were proposed to have 'strange quarks' in their composition.

Now let us revisit the 'beta decay' in the light of 'quark model'. As we know that during beta (β^-) decay, neutron transforms into proton. This conversion of neutron into proton brings change in the atomic number of the decaying nucleus from Z to (Z+1). After the arrival of quark theory, it is clear that the change of neutron into proton requires 'down' quark to get converted into 'up' quark. This is what is known as 'flavor change' by quarks. As beta decay is governed by weak interaction, we can say that the weak interaction changes the flavour of quarks. The flavour change results in 'nuclear transmutation'.

In this way, we see that only three quarks and four leptons were found sufficient to understand the emerging particle world so far. The 'troubling' hadrons are no more troubles now. Symmetry-loving physicists turned their attention in search of possible underlying symmetry between quarks and leptons.

Quark-lepton symmetry

Physicists have discovered many secrets of Nature, following the guidelines resulted from the symmetry. This belief led physicists to think that symmetry may also exist between the numbers of quarks and leptons. As we have seen, the building blocks of matter, the fermions, are four leptons and three quarks. One more quark was required in order to complete the symmetry.

Physicists had not to wait for long. Soon, one new particle was discovered by Burton Richter and his collaborators while studying collisions between beams of electrons and positrons. It was a new meson named as 'psi particle'. Being unaware of Richter's discovery, Samuel Ting also discovered a new meson in another experiment in which he directed proton beam on fixed target and called it 'J' particle. Later, both were shown to be the same particle. So, a due credit is given to both by calling this meson as 'J/psi' particle. It is this particle which required a new type of quark. It is the anticipated 'fourth' quark. It was named 'charm'. Like 'strangeness', the 'charm' is found to be a new property that remains conserved during the process. With this discovery, physicists were happy as they discovered what they expected to be present in Nature. The physicists found two lepton and two quark families. The most stable family members are the lowest mass members. These are 'electron and electron-neutrino' in lepton family and 'up and down quarks' in quark family. The heavier members in both the families have short life and decay into their respective stable members.

But suddenly the scene changed. Martin Lewis Perl and his team performed a series of 'electron-positron collision experiments' and discovered a new type of 'charged lepton' like electron and muon but much heavier (about 3500 times than that electron) than them. It was named 'tau'. Keeping in mind the earlier two families of leptons, the scientists put this in the new family called third family and predicted the existence of its corresponding neutral member tau-neutrino. This raised the number of leptons from four to six. The 'happy' quark-lepton symmetry got disturbed by this discovery.

In order to regain the desired quark-lepton symmetry, one more quark family of two quarks was now required. In order to discover these particles, physicists performed collision experiments at ultra-high energy. For these, the energetic proton beams were produced in the accelerator 'Tevatron' (which is also world's largest proton anti-proton collider) and discovered a new particle called 'upsilon' meson first. This meson required new quark for its existence. It has been given the name 'bottom' quark. This particle is known to possess a new property called 'beauty' that remained conserved during the process. The remaining member of this quark family is 'top' quark. Physicists were to wait for a long period of time to see its evidence in the laboratory but finally succeeded in discovering 'top' quark. The 'top' quark is as heavy as the nucleus of gold (forty time massive than the 'bottom' quark). It is characterized by a new property called 'truth' that remains conserved during the process. Now, physicists have evidences for 6 quarks and 5 leptons. Soon, the remaining sixth lepton 'tau-neutrino' was also discovered. The picture is stable and the symmetry seems to be completed with six leptons and six quarks with their anti-particles. All known material particles can be expressed in terms of these quarks and leptons. However, few questions still remain unanswered. Can there be a fourth family of quarks and leptons? Why do we have only three families, when only the lightest family members (up and down quarks) are necessary for understanding matter? What is the need of massive members in the family? ...

After meeting successes with quark model, physicists again turned their attention on the understanding of the fundamental interactions that govern the particle world.

Understanding interactions

As we have seen quantum electrodynamics (QED) is developed to understand electromagnetic interactions. It explains how matter interacts with electromagnetic field. It describes the interaction in terms of exchange of photon, the field particle. So, it is nothing but quantum field theory (QFT). Its success has been a great motivation. That's why it was natural for the physicists to extend QFT in nuclear domain. In this domain, nuclear strong and weak interactions dominate.

If we look at the interactions, we come to know that electron is influenced by both electromagnetic and weak interaction. But under 'normal' circumstances, electromagnetic interaction works over all distances whereas the weak nuclear interaction works only over very short distances. Abdus Salam with Sheldon Lee Glashow and Steven Weinberg developed theoretical models on the lines of QFT. They showed that these interactions become symmetric i.e. they remain no longer separate fields at temperatures above 10^{15}K (in terms of energy units, it is above

100 GeV). This unified field observed at high temperature is termed as 'electroweak' field. The field is governed by the exchange of mass-less 'field-boson'. The observed high-temperature symmetry breaks at low-temperature, resulting into two separate constituent fields, one governs long-range interaction (electromagnetic) through mass-less (photon) and other through massive (W^+, W^- and Z) bosons. These bosons have been predicted to possess masses around 100 times the mass of a proton! This appears to be unbelievable but principle of uncertainty and the theory of relativity make it possible'. Soon, Simon van der Meer and Carlo Rubbia discovered these bosons as per predictions. Thus, the unification scheme got experimentally confirmed. Physicists considered this as a major step in right direction and started moving forward in search of grand unification. But how does a mass-less field-boson acquire mass, during symmetry breaking, was puzzling. We will come on this issue later.

During this period, physicists also tried to understand the strong nuclear interactions. But QFT appeared to be a 'dead end' to understand. So, some physicists started with a fresh idea. To understand any process, two approaches are generally followed. They are 'top-down' and 'bottom-up' approaches. The QFD is 'top-down' approach. So, they thought to start with 'bottom-up' approach. This is bootstrap approach in which one computes scattering (s) – matrix directly without QFT. The s-matrix was proposed to obey certain properties abstracted away from QFT. The particles and interactions which emerge as the spectrum of the s-matrix from the scattering of states should be the same spectrum of particles that comes in as 'in-states'. They thought that all the consistency conditions were not yet discovered, and there might be many more. This thinking was convincing and inspirational too. It accommodates non-field theory of infinitely many particles without postulating the consistent particles like quarks and gluons as required in the top-down approach followed in QFT. The finite number of particle version of s-matrix theory is also a 'dead-end as it is found equivalent to QFT'. Then the idea of treating particles as 'string' emerged. String theory incorporates and gives concrete form to all bootstrap ideas. But then physicists following 'top-down' approach met brilliant success and created quantum chromodynamics (QCD). Naturally QCD took over and the idea of strings was cornered. Let us see how physicists found the path and created QCD.

QCD for nuclear strong force

Idea for the development of QCD has come from the observation of mysterious 'omega' particle. The structure of 'omega' particle has three 'strange' quarks. As mentioned earlier, the quarks are fermions and follow 'Pauli's exclusion principle'. So, the question arises, how can these three quarks occupy the same state? Now physicists have started building a logical story. They proposed quarks to be different and must possess some other specific property which can differentiate them. So, physicists associated 'colour charge' to the quarks. It must be remembered that the property 'colour' used in the quark theory is nothing to do with the visual perception of colour. Each quark is proposed to appear in 'red', 'yellow' and 'blue' colour. The 'colour' charge generates 'colour force' between the quarks, which is responsible for the binding of quarks inside baryons and mesons. The strong interaction observed between nucleons, as proposed by Yukawa, is like 'residual colour force' which extends 'beyond' nucleons but 'within' nuclear boundary. It is analogous to Vander Waals force that exists between atoms, which is residual electromagnetic force that exists between nucleus and the electrons inside the atom.

So far, all the efforts to observe 'free quarks' have failed. But quark-composites, mesons and baryons or hyperons, are observed freely. So, it is clear that quarks appear either in a group of two or three only. As no free quarks are available, physicists thought that the colour force that governs the interaction between the quarks is of different nature. Keeping this in mind, QCD is developed.

According to QCD, a continuous colour exchange takes place when two or more quarks are placed together. The interaction is practically zero and the quarks are totally free at zero-separation. But with increasing separation, the force between quarks increases, unlike other fields. This property of quarks is termed as 'asymptotic freedom'. This property is given the name 'Infrared Slavery'. Actually this special property of colour force imprisons the quarks within hadron-boundary never to be separated. Any effort to separate them requires energy. With increasing separation, the energy required to separate them farther any more also increases. Though energy supply increases, but the separation is not achieved. In fact, at one point of time the supplied energy to the particle reaches a value where energy gets converted into mass. So, instead of getting composite particles or sub-particles during collision, we may surprisingly get the same hadron as if the Nature denied to get herself exposed any more. There appeared a sign of question mark on further search. Will we not be in position to know the ultimate building block? Apart from this curiosity, the physicists looked the situation described above in a different way. It is as if the particle we have is behaving like a string with the quarks at its ends. When energy is supplied, it gets pulled. The string breaks into two pieces of four ends with four quarks at the ends. The energy supplied gets converted into mass under appropriate conditions. We will talk more on the idea of considering particles as string later in this book.

In QCD, the field-boson of the colour field is called 'gluon'. These gluons are massless, colour-charged and are eight in number. The gluons, comprised of units of colour and anti- colour, are bi-coloured. For example, the colour may be red anti-blue, blue-antired and so on. That's why; blue and red quarks interchange their colour by antiblue-red gluon. The exchange of red-antiblue gluon between red and blue quarks converts red gluon as blue and blue as red. Because of the presence of colour charge, the gluons interact with each other as well, giving non-zero probability of the existence of 'glue-balls'. In this sense, they are different from the massless photons, field boson of electromagnetic field.

In the light of QCD, a hadron (e.g. proton) is not a simple hadron but exists with enormous possibilities. Quarks present in them make 'white' combination. In colour terminology, three quarks (with red, green and blue) or two quarks (with colour and anti-color) make the groups 'white'. White groups exist freely. Inside the hadrons, exchange of gluon takes place between the quarks. During transit, particle-antiparticle (quark – antiquark) pairs are also created and annihilated continuously. So, logically, the hadrons may be pictured as made of fixed number of real quarks and surrounded by the gluons and virtual quark-antiquark cloud. Now let us apply the understanding to picture a collision event. In most collisions, the energy of the colliding particles goes in disrupting these clouds. As a result, the energy available may create new particles like 'W' and 'Z' bosons, which are known to govern weak interaction, capable for changing the flavour of quarks and thus the nature of nucleon (e.g. proton).

As we know, the colour force is confined within nucleonic boundaries only. This has extremely short range. But the QCD says its field-boson, gluon, to be massless. All other field-bosons involved in short range interactions like W^+, W^- and Z bosons are massive. In fact, the range of the interaction is directly related to the masses of field bosons, as suggested by uncertainty principle. Then, the natural question arises that why is 'gluon' behaving otherwise? Actually, the presence of colour charge on the massless gluons never allows them to leave the quark confining nucleonic boundary and limits their range. It may be recalled in this context that the photons are massless but have no electric charge on them making their range infinite.

Now the understanding of the constitution of matter is achieved. How particles interact with each other is also clear. It is also clear that at higher energies or at higher temperatures, diversities start vanishing as we have seen while developing electroweak theory and experimental confirmation of its predictions. We hope that at still higher energies, all other interactions will be unified and we will find evidence of unified single force. But, physicists were worried as they did not understand the mechanism through which the particles could gain mass. So, it was the last problem that they thought remained unanswered. The 'mass puzzle' was resolved by Peter Higgs who proposed the existence of Higgs field. A 'particle' acquires 'mass' by interacting with this field. Now the picture was clear and by including all these, a 'standard model' of matter was proposed. Let us see its salient features.

Standard Model

Standard model is developed to deal with particles and their interaction. It includes 12 fermions (6 of them are quarks and the rest are 6 leptons) and 5 gauge bosons, of which the one is gluon boson of 8-types. The quarks and leptons families were characterized as generations. The particles of generation-1 are less massive than the generation-2 particles. The generation-2 particles are less massive than generation-3 particles. Within generation the leptons are lighter than quarks and neutrinos are less massive than other leptons. In the standard model, the particles initially emerged as 'massless'. But, in the real universe, elementary particles possess a wide mass spectrum, ranging from massless to massive like gold nucleus. To account for the acquisition of mass by the particles, Higgs boson has been included in the model. With the discovery of Higgs boson in the year 2012, all predictions of the model were experimentally verified.

The model includes the QED and QCD to account the interactions involved in the particle world. The belief in symmetry suggests them to be a special case of some more fundamental and generalized theory. The field theories have many adjustable parameters or constants that could be put into the theory with any value we like. This was required to counter the problem of 'infinity'. So, the re-normalization techniques have been accepted as standard techniques in the model. The problem of infinity is related to the point-like structure of particles.

Though the model is successful in many respects, but it depends on 19 numerical parameters like mass of electron, mass of quarks, charge of electron etc. Their values are known from experiments but the origin of the values is unknown. The model however hints that extension of Salam and Weinberg's work on 'electroweak theory' should be possible. At higher energies the QCD should unite with electroweak theory in much the same way as electromagnetic theory unites with weak nuclear force theory. In this way, physicists expect to develop a grand unified theory (GUT). But 'gravity' still remains out of the scheme and poses a major challenge. Without the inclusion of gravity, we can't hope to get the theory of everything (TOE). The TOE should unite relativistic and quantum theories as well. The standard model seems to be a low-energy approximation to a more fundamental model. The model doesn't work above the energy where gravity cannot be ignored. The velocity dependence of mass must be remembered at this juncture. From the theory of relativity, we know that at velocity of light, the particle becomes infinitely massive. So, physicists looked back and revived the forgotten string theory, that emerged earlier during bootstrap thinking. In string theory, the particles are treated as strings in multi-dimensional space with multiple modes of vibration.

When string theory re-emerged in the scene, physicists turned their attention on the properties of strongly interacting particles. In an effort, they found some interesting features when they made angular 'momentum vs. mass-square' plots.

These are known as Regge trajectories. They noted that mesons gave same slopes for the trajectories. The Regge trajectories that determine high energy scattering are called 'pomerons'. The pomeron in string theory becomes the closed string which includes 'graviton', giving hope for the gravity to be included in the theoretical framework. The relationship between the closed string and QCD pomeron is a subject of active research today.

Further, the standard model was found to be inadequate in explaining some astrophysical observations related to the total matter present in the universe. Observations suggest that only about 4 percent of the total matter present in the universe is baryonic in nature. The rest of the matter is speculated to be in the form of 'dark matter' and 'dark energy'. This model presents no any suitable particle that can resolve the matter puzzle of the universe.

In spite of all the above mentioned inadequacies, the standard model is a grand success in the 'low-energy' limits. At present, physicists are trying to go beyond this model, where much new physics is expected to emerge. We are to wait and watch!

5

UNIVERSE - NEW VISION!

The universe is full of mysteries and puzzles. In order to understand it we have to rely on clues as most of the heavenly objects are beyond our physical reach. The only clue available to us is the 'light' that connects us with the stellar objects. We have seen earlier how beautifully, the analysis of 'light' has guided us in disclosing the secrets of the material world at microscopic level. The same 'light' also helped us in knowing a lot about the past, present and future of the vast universe spread before us.

The physicists, while working in the laboratories, realized that the colour of light emitted by the 'hot objects' can provide a clue to determine its 'temperature'. They noticed that with rising temperature, the body changes its colour in going from 'red-hot' to 'white-hot' state. On heating further, especially the materials having high melting point, appear blue. Physicist Wilhelm Wien studied in great detail and found a law that relates the emission characteristics of the black bodies with their temperature. Assuming stellar bodies as black bodies, physicists used Wein's law and estimated the temperature of stars. Initial classification was made on the basis of surface temperature as estimated from this law. The stars are classified as M (red, with temperature less than 3500K), K (yellow-orange), G (yellow), F (yellow-white), A (white), B (blue-white) and O (blue with temperature more than 30000K). For near-stars, the idea worked nicely. But for low-intensity distant-stars, physicists faced problems. Then they started looking into the details of stellar spectra and identified certain prominent absorption lines corresponding to the presence of certain ions. Ionization and temperature are inherently related. So physicists logically found indirect way of knowing the temperature of any star. After the realization that the knowledge of temperatures, sizes, luminosities and distances from earth may help them in knowing the structural features of stars, the spectral analysis of the stellar light became the main area of activity. Some physicists made spectral classifications of stars.

Physicists Ejnar Herztsprung and Henry Norris Russell studied these classifications and discovered independently a relationship between the brightness of a star and the spectral type. They made a plot between 'luminosity' and 'spectral type' and observed that most of the stars occupied the region in the diagram along a line. This represents the 'main sequence'. Stars of greater luminosity were toward the top of the diagram, and stars with higher surface temperature were toward the left side of the diagram. But the diagram also showed some 'blue stars' having low luminosity and 'red stars' with high luminosity. These have been taken as suggestions by physicists about the possible demonstration of stellar evolution! Physicists also inferred from this observation that stars live a life and a star moves up or down along the line of the main sequence in the course of their lifetimes! In other words, the study of 'H-R diagram' gave them a suggestion that stars at the end of their life may get collapsed. They may finally appear as 'red giants' or 'dwarf stars'. Now, physicists turned their attention in knowing the stellar constituents and the source that keeps them burning all through their life.

People in ancient and medieval periods were having no idea about the material that constitutes heavenly bodies. But when physicists identified materials by studying their spectral fingerprints, work in this direction began. Physicists collected spectral data in order to know their constituent materials. 'Hydrogen', the lightest element, emerged as a main constituent material of all stars. 'Helium' was the next. All other natural elements also indicated their presence.

The intensity of the spectral fingerprint of atoms tells about the abundance of the materials. More the abundance, more intense the fingerprint is. During the spectral studies of the sun, the presence of 'calcium ion' was found in a region where the temperature was not enough to ionize calcium. This observation was quite puzzling and unexpected! Meghnad Saha, a young teacher from India turned his attention to this issue. Contrary to the existing belief, he thought that it is not only the 'temperature variations' but also the 'pressure variations' that are responsible for bringing changes in the state of ionization of an element in a star. He then proposed the 'ionization equation', now known after his name. It provided a basis that relates the spectral classes of stars to their surface temperatures. Further, as an atom or ion can absorb or emit radiation of a particular set of wavelengths, the intensity of the spectral set in the stellar spectrum is directly related to the relative numbers of atoms or ions it contains. Saha's theory also helped in determining the elemental abundances in the stars. This equation has thus become as one of the basic tools in astrophysical studies.

The spectral studies have been found quite useful in knowing many other properties of stars. By now, it was established beyond doubt that the sun is at very high temperature and the matter therein is in ionized form i.e., in the 'plasma' state. Physicists could know about the existence of stellar magnetic fields. It could be possible after the discovery of Zeeman Effect. According to this effect, the energy levels of atoms and ions are split into more than one level in the presence of a magnetic field. This 'Zeeman splitting' of spectral lines has been observed in solar spectrum. This indicated the presence of magnetic field in the sun. During these studies, physicists also discovered the regions of lower temperatures and stronger magnetic fields than the surroundings. These were named 'sunspots'. The sunspots have been found to be related with solar activities. With increasing number of sunspots, solar activity increases. They further noticed that their number varies giving 'maxima' approximately after 11 years. This indicated that the matter in the sun is highly dynamic. The sunspot cycle indicated that the matter in the sun rotates as well. Actually the solar magnetic field observed results from the motion of the ionized matter. The same argument is applicable for other stellar objects.

In this creative period, Subramanian Chandrasekhar got attracted in the theory of evolution of stars, especially of 'white dwarf', the ultimate fate of sun-like stars. It was the time when atomic structure was clear and quantum theory was proving to be a new effective tool to understand the nature at micro-level. The stellar objects are at very high temperature and pressure. Under these conditions, matter appears in plasma state, in which nuclei and electrons are freely available. Thus, he innovatively thought of using quantum ideas to the physics of stellar structures. He realized that when a star like the sun exhausts its nuclear fuel available in the form of hydrogen, it stops producing energy. The material left now is in the form of helium ions and electrons. The gravitation pulls the material towards the centre but it doesn't work for electrons beyond certain limit. The limit is set by the special property of the electrons, which is governed by Pauli's exclusion principle. This principle prevents electrons from getting too close to one another and they form degenerate electron-gas. This creates 'degeneracy pressure' in the direction opposite to that of gravitation. When equilibrium is established, a new category of star appears. Chandrasekhar calculated that the stars less than 1.44 solar masses stabilize as 'white dwarf'. But more massive stars beyond this 'limit' become 'neutron stars' or 'black holes'. Thus, it has become clear that after living a life stars die.

Interest in cosmology led physicists to discover many mysterious and surprising facts of Nature. Simple telescopes developed for visible range also guided to develop new types of telescopes with new detection techniques in other spectral ranges like radio waves, microwaves, infrared, ultraviolet, x-rays etc. The space was scanned thoroughly. New clues were obtained to understand the universe. The proofs for the birth and death of a star were collected. The evidences for white dwarfs, neutron stars and black holes were found. The luminous variable stars 'Cepheids' have been found and identified as new 'yard stick' to measure the astronomical distances. With further understanding, some other yard sticks (resulting from stellar explosions in binary system known as supernovae type 1a) were also discovered. It's all interesting and seems to be unbelievable but it is a reality.

Let us now come on the issue of stellar energy. What may be its source?

What keeps stars burning?

Initially 'chemical combustion' was thought to be a possible source of stellar energy (energy from the sun is termed solar energy). Though attractive, the idea was rejected as the process would burn away the entire sun in few thousand years. We know that the sun is shining and giving light continuously for billions of years. So, physicists thought that the solar energy must be produced in a radically different way. And, surely it should not by combining various elements by normal chemical processes, but by producing new chemical elements as suggested by the spectroscopic analysis. In this process, the mass must be converted into energy in accordance with Einstein's mass-energy relation. Let us see how can it be possible?

It has been mentioned earlier that in the stellar bodies like the sun, temperature and pressure are very high and so the matter existing there is in plasma form. The conditions in the 'stellar core' are quite suitable for the fusion of lighter nuclei like that of hydrogen present there. Physicist Francis William Aston with his 'mass spectrograph' made precise measurements of different atoms. He found that four individual hydrogen nuclei were more massive than a helium nucleus consisting of four nuclear particles. It was here that the physicists recalled Einstein's mass-energy equivalence formula, originated from his theory of relativity. It seemed that hydrogen nuclei are getting converted into helium and releasing 'difference in masses' in the form of energy. The physicists speculated that the process should be very slow in order to allow the sun to shine for billions of years. It was the time when the 'atomic nucleus' was discovered but not much was known about the 'nuclear processes'. However, after the discovery of neutron, physicists had sufficient information about the atomic nucleus. They calculated the details of how hydrogen can fuse to become helium. For getting helium, two protons and two neutrons are required. So in order to get helium, first requirement is to obtain neutrons from the available hydrogen nuclei i.e. protons. The conversion of proton into neutron is governed by the then newly discovered weak nuclear force.

Interestingly, the process of the conversion of a proton into neutron is extremely slow and so the energy generation process in a star can continue for billions of years as desired to match with other geological and biological evidences. The initial contributions of physicists Hans Bethe and Carl von Weizsäcker are very important in developing these ideas.

In this way the spectroscopy, the knowledge of nuclear forces and Einstein's theory of relativity helped physicists in disclosing the secret of stellar energy. They proposed 'thermonuclear fusion in the stellar core' as the only viable operative 'mechanism'.

Now, let us concentrate on another important issue that is related to the origin of the universe. For this, physicists made painstaking efforts in order to get some more information contents in the light spread all along the space. Some astonishing observations were made that led them to understand the origin of universe.

Probably Universe was born!

Edwin Hubble was interested in stellar spectroscopy. He observed 'red shift' (shift of the entire set of spectral lines in the spectrum towards low frequency side) in the spectra of various galaxies. Doppler Effect can be used to understand this observation. This effect tells us how the frequency of light (and sound) depends upon the 'relative' motion between source and detector. Most of us are familiar with this effect when we hear 'difference in frequency' of sound of a car or a train as it moves toward or away from us. In the present case as the observation of spectral red shift is made from our galaxy, Doppler Effect suggests that the galaxy under observation is moving away from us. This understanding works for other galaxies too. As none of the observations gave 'blue shift' (shift of the entire set of spectral lines in the spectrum towards high frequency side), Hubble concluded that all galaxies are moving away from us. Further, as we are not at any special location, the same 'shift' must be observed from any other space location too. It means all the galaxies are moving away from each other. This helps in concluding logically that the universe is expanding! It suggests that the galaxies were closer in the past and occupied less space. Further, there must be moment in the past, when all the matter of the galaxies must have been concentrated at a point and we would have had a 'point-universe'! Then under favourable conditions (we don't know how and why as it is quantum territory), it must have started expanding rapidly giving birth to the present universe. In technical language, the moment of creation is "Big Bang"! George Gamow developed a theory using thermodynamics by considering the universe to be a 'black body'. He predicted that the universe is continuously cooling since its birth as adiabatic conditions prevailed. According to him, the temperature of the universe, at present, should be around 2.65K, which at the beginning was 10^{20}K. Arno Penzias and Robert Wilson discovered weak radio signals (in the microwave range) coming from all parts of the sky and the spectrum matched to that of a black body at the temperature predicted by Gamow. This is recognized as the 'remnant' of the very hot radiation from the Big Bang that created the universe about 13 billion years ago. It appeared perfectly 'symmetric' and no 'inhomogeneity' was noticed. So naturally the question arose; how galaxies were created? Where are the seeds of galaxies? For the creation of galaxies, 'temperature inhomogeneity' is required to exist. So, efforts began in this direction. 'Cosmic Background Explorer' (COBE) satellite and 'Wilkinson Microwave Anisotropy Probe' satellite missions were undertaken. They carried sensitive instruments to measure minute fluctuations in temperature. The missions were successful. A 'stencil' was found which is possibly used to create the universe. Study of the 'cosmic microwave background radiation' in greater detail over the entire sky is in progress.

Matter puzzle! New proposals

Astronomer Vera Rubin observed some strange results like the stars moved at similar speeds throughout the 'Andromeda' galaxy. She obtained similar results while studying 200 other galaxies. It was beyond her expectation. Actually she anticipated that the stars in the outer part should orbit at a slower rate compared to those located near the central region of the galaxy. This is what we observe for the planets of our solar system. Interestingly, Fritz Zwicky had also got this result earlier. It proved to be a breakthrough which revealed that there's far more mass out than was previously suspected, not detectable by our instruments directly but affecting the gravity. It may interest us to know that normal material that we can detect with our instruments or see with our eyes is called 'baryonic matter' and is only about 4%. The remaining 96 % is unaccountable.

Today, physicists have developed theories to explain the origin of unaccountable matter. They firmly believe that there exists some unknown kind of 'dark matter' that surrounds the galaxies needed to explain what Vera Rubin observed. Estimation shows the 'dark matter' to be about 23% of the total mass of the universe. Further the universe is expanding at accelerated pace. This requires energy to counter gravitational attraction. Physicists believe that this could be possible if the remaining 73 percent of the mass of the Universe is present in the form of 'dark energy'. No any experiment has yet been performed that proves the presence of dark energy. So, these are speculations. There may be other possible explanations!

Neutrino – New window to peep in the universe

As described earlier, while solving the puzzle of beta decay (one of the decay mode of radioactive nuclei), 'neutrino' was proposed to be emitted along with beta particle. It is produced at all the places where nucleon transformation takes place. In the sun's core, fusion takes place that converts hydrogen into helium. But for this, first a neutron is to be converted into proton. It is this process, during which neutrino is produced. Neutrino interacts very-very weakly with matter and so it comes out without any hindrance, unlike a photon. Photon that interacts very strongly with matter, takes about 40 thousand years in coming out of the sun. So what is happening inside the sun can be known by the study of neutrinos without delay as it takes only the time that required completing the flight. In this way, neutrino provides a 'new window' to look at the universe and the data may be used to make predictions. Huge labs and observatories were constructed in order to study the neutrinos coming from the sun, galactic cores and supernovae in detail.

While studying solar neutrinos, scientists met a puzzling result. The solar neutrinos received were only one third of the predicted number. Where can the remaining two-third go? At the beginning of their journey from the sun, they were of one flavour. But during the journey, they changed their flavour and so at the detector a mixture of three flavours is recorded. As the initial set-ups were established to record only one flavour the results appeared puzzling. The flavour changing property of neutrinos is termed as 'neutrino oscillation'. The physicists noted that the flavour change of neutrino is governed by the change in the mass. This is quite surprising and strange as neutrinos were believed to be mass-less. This brought change at the conceptual level. Today, the neutrino is amongst one of the potential candidates that can contribute to the 'dark matter' in the universe.

PART-IV

Vicissitudinal Vistas

6

NEW ROADS: NEW CHALLENGES

After the advent of Maxwell's electromagnetic theory, Einstein's theory of relativity and Schrodinger-Heisenberg-Dirac's quantum mechanics, Mathematics has emerged a most powerful tool to explore relationships. For quantum pioneers, no picture seemed necessary to be made. Twentieth century physics tells us to follow mathematics as guiding force! We may land in the unknown and unexplored territory with the help of mathematics! There is a clear message: believe in what mathematics says, make predictions confidently and let the experimentalists verify them. Further, after experimental confirmation, let the technologists exploit them.

The development of quantum mechanical theory raised the question on the nature of 'reality'. The champions Bohr and Heisenberg were of the opinion that reality takes birth only at the time of measurement. Their argument was based on 'Copenhagen interpretation' of the wave function. According to this, the quantum system exists in all probable states before measurement. When one measures, all but one states collapses. Thus, the measurement creates 'reality'. However, this strange kind of nature of reality doesn't appeal to common sense and so, pioneers like

Einstein and Schrodinger were against this argument. According to Einstein 'reality' exists since birth before the actual measurements are made and so he talked about the incompleteness of quantum mechanics and suggested about the existence of some hidden variables. The issue didn't get settled and so a debate is initiated on the nature of reality. At one occasion, when Einstein made a remark that God doesn't play dice', Bohr counter replied by saying 'don't tell God what to do and what not'. Einstein had no answer to that at that time but then Einstein wrote a paper, famous as EPR (Einstein, Podolsky and Rosen) paper, on the basis of a 'thought experiment' to counter Bohr. Both the camps were biased. The debate continued but without any conclusion. But the physicists, in general, were happy because quantum mechanics was yielding the fruits. Actually the developments brought 'first quantum revolution'. This was the reason that nobody was willing to waste (or invest) time in considering questions about the very basic concepts at work in quantum mechanics. So, the debate was side-lined because of its philosophical and not technological importance. The issue continued and gave technological fruits for sufficiently long period. But later in 1960s, when John Bell entered in the scene, the unsettled issue of reality emerged again.

The main hypothesis of Bell's work (theorem) is based on Einstein's view that the strange quantum effects can be explained by some hidden variables and the correlations between the two entangled particles are established at the source. If the theorem is valid, then every action is predetermined, as properties are assigned at the time of birth of pair. Bell established some inequalities and suggested a way to resolve the issue through 'single particle interference' experiments. First series of experiments started with neutrons. These were initiated by Helmut Rauch in 1974. Some large molecules like fullerenes produce interference effects. Other molecules like insulin and some bio-molecules are in line to exhibit interference phenomena. In these experiments, the particle is allowed to pass through 'double slit system' like that used by Young. The interference pattern is observed. But it is possible only when the particle behaves like a quantum system and exhibits wave-like characteristics.

In 1985, Alain Aspect met the condition of getting single 'photon' at a time. He found interference effects with single photon. This clearly indicated that the particle must have passed through both the slits (by getting delocalized) and all the particles remain in communication with each other (by getting entangled) irrespective of the distance between them. Further, in these experiments, the interference is observed only when one doesn't try to know which path the particle is following. If one interrupts and tries to know the actual path followed by the particle, the interference pattern disappears. It means the 'reality' takes birth at the time of observation. Before this, nothing can be said about the path the particle has followed. This shows that the Nature cannot be described according to Einstein's view-point. Actually, the act of observation affects the reality and so nothing can be said about the particle's reality before measurement.

Single-particle interference experiments gave us new guiding principles in the form of 'non-locality' and 'entanglement' to understand quantum world. This new understanding triggered 'second quantum revolution'. This offers completely new possibilities in the domain of information treatment and transmission. A new age of quantum information through 'quantum binary logic' began. Though challenging, quantum computing is no longer a far-dream now. In today's digital world, quantum cryptography (in which a secret key can be shared between any two persons without any interference by the third person) has already been put to use for safe transactions.

At this place, it is worth mentioning the newly emerging area of bio-photonics. It deals with the emission from living cells. Alexander Gurwitsch was the first scientists who indirectly gave evidence of this emission in 1923. But a real breakthrough came in 1970, when Fritz Albert Popp, provided conclusive evidences of this bio-photonic emission and showed it to be clearly different from 'chemi-luminescence' (light-emitting reactions as observed in the firefly or jellyfish) and 'delayed fluorescence'. This emission is electromagnetic in nature and is influenced greatly by the biological factors like temperature change, oxygen supply etc. and also by the physiological processes. There is a strong correlation between 'cell division' rate in the living organism and its bio-photon intensity. Further, it is observed that the more complex the organism, the fewer photons were emitted. In a stressed state, the rate of bio-photon emission goes up. The bio-photon emission drops for normal cell populations with increasing cell density, but opposite behaviour is observed for the cancer cells. Similar behaviour is observed while measuring the degree of coherence of bio-photonic emission. Popp studied the bio-emission theoretically and proposed that DNA should act as a 'store house' of light and should be responsible for the observed emission from the living cells. The study showed coherent nature of the bio-emission. So, DNA in each living cell is proposed to act as a 'bio-laser'. Popp applied the idea in order to understand 'intra' and 'inter' cellular communication. He proposed DNA as an 'information tool' and a perfect communicator that encodes and transfers information. This research has recently motivated the scientists to look into the possible role of junk DNA in the body. New results are baffling and need much attention.

New challenges! Yet to learn!!

Scientists have solved so many different types of puzzles. We have seen that in past the puzzling black lines in solar spectrum were nothing but the signatures of the atoms present in the sun. This basic knowledge helped us in understanding the constitution of all stars and galaxies. The puzzling observation of radioactivity was really the call from the tiny nucleus sitting inside atom. When the puzzle was solved, we came to know about two new types of fundamental interactions. While understanding puzzling beta decay, neutrino's existence was hypothesized. The radioactive materials are characterized by their half-life. This characteristic made them natural time-keepers. 'Half-life' is the period during which half of the original radioactive nuclei get disintegrated. However, it is a mystery that if all the nuclei are identical, then why do certain nuclei get disintegrate faster than others. And, also why does in long-run, a single nucleus remain 'immortal' and never gets disintegrated. There is no answer. Life in itself is a great puzzle and mystery. There are few more mysteries that are posing serious challenges to the physicists today. The most important one amongst them is related to disappearance of antimatter after the birth of universe. Our curious mind wants to know the answers to some of the questions like what was before big bang; as the universe is expanding, is it going to become ultra-low freeze? What is total mass/energy of the universe? Is the total energy of the universe is zero, as all positive energy (in the form of matter and energy) is equal to the negative energy stored in the gravitational energy? Are the universal constants really constant? What may be the physics beyond standard model? Are we living in multi-dimensional universe as suggested by superstring theories? And many more such questions…

Challenges - 'would be science' areas

Some challenges are also coming from the 'would be science' areas like paranormal and homeopathy. Some people claim to have entirely different connections with the world around them. Some believe that they can see directly into the future, or discover what someone else is experiencing kilometers away. They are called 'extra sensory' or 'paranormal' because the ability claimed cannot involve ordinary senses. A great Hindu Yogi Yoganand has written a detailed paranormal account of his life in his famous book 'Autobiography of a Yogi'. It is difficult even to decide whether these claims are mere accidental, simply fake, or right. So before accepting or rejecting them, physicists should make sure that all the factors causing mistakes and fraud have positively been ruled out. Some experiments related to the paranormal experiences have been performed under controlled conditions in a scientific way. Though the results are not conclusive, but they do seriously demand explanations. Similarly, homeopathy is coming up as a very significant type of alternative medicine system. In case of injury, some specific remedies like 'arnica *montana*', 'hypericum *perforatum*', 'rhustoxicodendron' in very high dilutions, work so miraculously that one is forced to think seriously about the mode of action of these medicines. I myself tried and experimented number of times the curative effects unfailingly. So, the success of homeopathy is posing serious challenges to the physicists. The only clue available at this time is the symptom it produces in the human body. It suggests that the homeopathic medicines should have some sort of 'bio-identification' mark recognizable by the mind of the patient in addition to its well-established 'electronic identification'. But all these observations fall in the category of 'subjective' experiences. Physics is an 'objective science' till now. It has no room for subjective experiences. But the real subjective experiences point towards the limitations and incompleteness of our present day's scientific knowledge. So, there exists a real challenge before physicists to extend the boundaries of physics. It is here, we feel that today physics is in similar dilemma as classical physics was in the late 19th century. The twentieth century physics has emerged from the existing clues but in unconventional ways. It is the period, when physicists have begun to loosen their way of rigid thinking. So, what may be the new direction this time? Will the new interpretation of quantum and relativity physics be closer to that of spirituality? Will physics marry psychology to incorporate subjective experiences? The curiosity now is centered on the question 'is there any need to expand the boundaries or need to create new physics!

Hopes…

In the last century, while solving the puzzling issues physicists discovered some new universal constants which were required to solve the puzzle of the universe. The concepts of space and time have thoroughly been revised and were found to be 'elastic' under relativistic conditions.

Not only this, they have been found to be interconnected. The relativity also made matter and energy as equivalent quantities. At quantum level, the language of probability and uncertainty has become important. The universe now appeared indeterminate and inseparable into parts. It appeared utterly strange to our common sense. But when experimental evidences started pouring in, they confirmed that the world is much more 'magical' and 'bizarre' than anticipated in nineteenth century. With new quantum and relativity physics, the seemingly impossible started looking possible. Michio Kaku, a theoretical physicist has described many far-fetched ideas which are destined to become the reality in near and far future in his book 'Physics of the impossible'. Kaku described three classes of impossibilities with classical physics point of views. His class I includes the impossibilities (like telepathy, psychokinesis, invisibility etc.), which do not violate known laws of physics but his class II are the impossibilities (like time machine, travel through worm hole etc.), which are the outcome of our today's understanding of the physical world. Interestingly his class III impossibilities included the technologies that violate the known laws of physics. Many subjective experiences fall in this category. It is here Kaku feels that if they do not turn out to be possible from the present physics, then they would give rise to a fundamental shift in our understanding of physics.

Let us get inspired and move in the unexplored territory of physics which can convert today's impossibilities into tomorrow's possibilities. But to enter in the world of physics, we require a lot of inspirations. For this we may go through the autobiographies of scientists. Once we enter in this world, we discover many such points wherefrom not only the technologies but messages can also be extracted to live a meaningful life.

PART –V

INSPIRATIONS AND MESSAGES

7

INSPIRATIONS

Creative persons get self-inspired by the desire to achieve or to become different than others. It is their desire that drives them to do something non-conventional and special. But, at many occasions, there are hindrances and we struggle to find sources of inspiration to move. However, there is a wide-range of sources that may provide us inspirations. Even ordinary hard working individuals living in our neighbourhoods may inspire us. But we fail to notice their presence.

An 'instant help' may be provided by the 'history' of science. Here, we find many great and influential scientists, who spent their lives for the cause of science. With less facilities and technologies, they could perform unimaginable experiments and developed theories by accepting the challenges and taking risks even of their lives. So to remain inspired, we need to focus on the way they followed to achieve and create science. More we focus and think about the way they struggled, more inspired we feel.

Physics is a creative science. Its growth depends on continuous questioning and finding answers. Getting answer and remaining curious is not easy. We may come across the hours of crisis and depression. During these hours, we may think about those scientists, who left their comfort zones, worked and created new things, gave new ideas and better understanding, created new theories and found new relationships. 'Thinking this way' may provide us a great help in the moments of despair.

The biographies of scientists really inspire a lot because we learn from them about their commitment and dedication. We also learn from them about how they committed mistakes and learned from them. While reading their biographies, a desire to become like them inspires us. This pumps energy that triggers thoughts like 'I need to learn how to do, understand and find solutions'. Biographies really help us in understanding the inner working of the minds of scientists and the creative processes they adopted during their scientific journey. The knowledge of the impact of their research and experiences may motivate us to do something impressive. Biographies provide us the techniques to train our minds. Trained mind becomes the imaginative mind that is needed to explore the connectivity between thoughts and new relationships.

If we go through history of science and biographies of scientists, we learn how 'Archimedes' worked to solve the scientific problems he met. We also learn how 'Galileo' questioned 'Aristotle' and how he answered many questions by performing experiments. Biographies tell us how 'Faraday' influenced 'Maxwell' and 'Maxwell' influenced 'Einstein'. Einstein's imaginative and creative mind performed thought experiments, whose results changed the course of Physics in the twentieth century. There are numerous such examples.

In what follows, we find a list of scientists who are the great source of inspiration. We may suitably get plugged in and confidently enter in the world of physics.

Archimedes

Archimedes is known as a great inventor, mathematician, physicist and engineer in the history of science. His statement that 'give me a place to stand on, and I will move the earth' shows about the level of confidence he possessed. He really had a great ability to think logically and creatively.

His 'eureka' comes at the lips during any 'enlightening moment' even today. There is famous anecdote about the word, 'eureka'. According to it, he was asked by the king to check the purity of gold used in his crown without damaging it. Archimedes was finding no clue. All of sudden, while swimming in a pond he got the idea. He noticed that water level rose on his getting into the pond. He suddenly got 'enlightenment'. Idea clicked and he found a technique to answer. He was so happy that he ran naked on the streets shouting Eureka, Eureka! It became a great contribution. Physicists got a handy technique of determining the volume of objects of any shape. From the density of the material, corresponding volume is known. On comparing with the measured volume, one can determine the purity of the material.

Archimedes is a great source of inspiration for persons of all ages. His biography tells us that we may be enlightened even in most common hours. The message is clear that the best science can come effortlessly, if we are focused, deeply involved and fully concerned.

Galileo Galilei

If we look at the history of Galileo's time, we will find none of his height and caliber. He was a thorough observer and logical thinker. He is known as a physicist, mathematician, astronomer and philosopher. He revolutionized experimental scientific methods that brought 'objectivity' in science. When he had doubt on the belief that heavier objects fall faster than lighter ones, he performed an experiment by dropping two spheres of different weights from the top of the Leaning Tower of Pisa and proved objectively that the belief was wrong. He thus gave a clear message not to accept anything by its face-value or because some respectable person has told it. His teaching is very clear that do experiment and then accept what you observe.

Once, Galileo visited a church. There he carefully noticed that a suspended swinging lamp was making periodic to and fro motion. It caught his attention. Ideas started pouring in. He made a systematic study and discovered the characteristics features of pendulum that gave him an idea to measure time intervals. Later, a pendulum clock was invented by Christiaan Huygens. Great physicist of all time Isaac Newton also got inspired by his experiments on projectiles and led him to investigate all types of motions in detail. Galileo invented a telescope to study the heavens and succeeded in making many important discoveries which laid the foundation of modern astronomy.

Galileo, who proposed that the centre of universe is not 'the earth' but the sun around which, along with other planets, the earth itself revolves, commanded a lot of respect in public. His observations made him confident about making such statements in public. But it was against the belief of Church and so he was ordered life-time imprisonment. He accepted this even in his old age but never bowed down. For the sake of truth, he did not hesitate to accept imprisonment.

We can draw a lot of inspirations from Galileo's life. How keen and careful observations can make us different is the lesson that we can learn from him. According to his biographers, the observation of cosmic event 'supernova' (it appears when a massive star explodes) in 1604, kindled his interest in observational astronomy while his visits to sea sites near city Venice, created interest in science. There's a lot in Galileo that inspires us.

Isaac Newton

Inspired by Frances Bacon, René Descartes, Edmund Halley and Galileo Galilei, Isaac Newton is known as all-time genius. His 'Principia', which gives an account of mathematical principles of natural philosophy, is the most revered book. His contributions are numerous and in varied fields like, mechanics, sound, heat, optics, astronomy and mathematics. His 'laws of motion' are most fundamental building blocks and are guiding forces for anybody interested in science. His contribution in mathematics, especially 'calculus' is a mandatory mathematical tool required to analyze most of the physical problem. His works on 'motion' and 'light' are highly innovative. His experiment to prove that white light is a mixture of light of different colours, led the foundation of 'spectroscopy'.

Newton's contributions are un-parallel in the history of science. His discoveries and inventions led science for nearly 300 years. He was a source of inspiration to many, including Albert Einstein. Einstein revived his idea of corpuscular nature of light and created 'quantum theory of light'.

Newton's words, 'I was like a boy playing on the seashore and diverting myself now and then finding a smoother pebble or a prettier shell than ordinary, whilst the great ocean of truth lay all undiscovered before me' inspires a lot.

James Clerk Maxwell

Maxwell is most influential physicist in the history of physics. He was very curious and intelligent. He discovered the predictive power of any theory that is based on strong logics. From his very childhood, he used to apply his curiosity to simple scientific investigations. One may not believe that his first scientific paper appeared when he was just 15. Later in life, he started working in getting a unified theoretical picture to show that magnetism, electricity and light are the manifestation of the same basic laws. His theory became one of the foundation stones of physics. Departing from Newton's view, the conceptual changes that he brought soon initiated wide range of developments in the field of communication and revolutionized information and communication systems. The world-wide-web that we have today would have not been possible without his theory.

Maxwell brought changes in the axiomatic basis of physics. His theory has not only guided the experimentalists to set their agenda but also gave invitation to theoretical physicists to explore some unknown territories logically. Albert Einstein was greatly inspired and deeply impressed by him. He has used the outcome of Maxwell's theory in form of constancy of the velocity of light for the development of his most revolutionary 'theory of relativity'. Maxwell lives in the heart of engineers and scientists and continues inspiring them.

Albert Einstein

Albert Einstein is known as today's greatest mysterious brain, which influenced not only the physicists but also many others from diverse areas. His contributions changed the very foundation of physics to an unbelievable extent. Differing from Galileo, he brought 'observer' in the central place of the stage of physics. His words 'we can't solve problems by using the same kind of thinking we used when we created them' guide new-comers in science.

Einstein was a great admirer of Isaac Newton, Michael Faraday and James Clerk Maxwell. He experienced a deep sense of wonder for the first time when he saw the magnetic compass. That time, he was aged only five. Later, 'Euclidean plane geometry' influenced him and had indescribable influence on him. Actually, geometry had always remained in the core of his thinking. Immanuel Kant's 'The Critique of Pure Reason' created life-long interest in him for philosophy. He believed in the 'principle of equivalence of physical laws' and the result on the 'constancy of velocity of light'. This led him to discover the fact that all physical quantities, including that of space and time are relative. His unusual way of thinking led him to present energy and mass on same footing. The equation '$E = mc^2$' soon became his icon. His wild imagination made us realize that we live in four dimensional 'space-time' world. After this, Einstein got the idea of explaining the origin of gravitation. It was in terms of curvature of space-time.

He was very clear in his thinking. It made him confident and bold. He never hesitated in proposing any non-conventional idea or logical thought. When he realized that in order to understand photoelectric effect, quantum nature of light is essential but to understand interference, wave nature, he took no time in making a proposal that light possesses 'dual nature' i.e. it behaves like a wave as well as particle. Both the natures are complementary to each other. Einstein's idea inspired Luis de Broglie. Importance of symmetry was apparent. Like radiation, matter may also possess dual nature! In this way, de Broglie's 'matter wave' hypothesis took birth. This work inspired Ervin Schrödinger, who discovered 'wave mechanics' to deal with micro-world.

Einstein's deep understanding of atomic processes led him to propose two types of emissions, 'spontaneous' and 'stimulated'. His idea of stimulated emission got materialized and we saw the birth of 'maser' (microwave amplification by stimulated emission of radiation) and 'laser' (light amplification by stimulated emission of radiation). His dream of 'unification of fundamental forces' has drawn the agenda of physics. He is a great source of inspiration not only for the present generation but for the generations to come.

Satyendra Nath Bose

Bose is all-time great physicist. He is one of the architects of 'New Physics'. A class of elementary particles is known after his name as Boson'. When Higg's Boson was recently discovered, he was remembered with great respect and admiration.

Bose was a mathematical genius. He got inspired by Einstein in his young age. After joining physics department of Calcutta University as a lecturer, he in collaboration with Meghnad Saha translated Einstein's theory of relativity from German to English for wider use. Later, he derived Planck's law by treating light as massless, indistinguishable and identical particles. Einstein got impressed by the work and was able to see its versatility. He extended and elaborated his statistics into a new form, which is now known as Bose Einstein statistics. The theory predicted a new coherent state of matter, BEC (Bose Einstein Condensate), at ultra-low temperature. It took about 60 years to verify the prediction. Today, BEC is a new area of activity and has given birth to 'atom optics'. The atom lasers have already been developed. The atom-laser is the atomic analogy to the optical laser, producing a coherent beam of matter waves rather than a coherent beam of light. Today, Bose is a source of great inspiration for the original thinkers.

Joseph Von Fraunhofer

Joseph Von Fraunhofer was a son of a poor glassmaker. He started working quite early, at the age of 10, in his father's glass workshop. So he received very little formal education. At the age of 11, he lost his parents and he was forced to pass his days in hardship. On one day when he was sleeping, the workshop collapsed and he was buried in the ruins but was saved. He took this as an opportunity and continued honing his skills further. Soon, he got reputation in making 'achromatic lenses' and developing precision optical instruments required for astronomical works. The quality of the instruments was so good that he started getting 'orders' in good number that improved his financial health. For calibrating the instruments, he used to employ conventional bright candles. But Fraunhofer remained watchful, creative and innovative while working. One day, out of sheer interest, he chose the 'sun' and not the 'candle' for calibration. It is this move that became the most historic transformative move in the history of science. He got solar spectrum which showed unusual 'partitions' i.e. black lines. Upon improving the technique further, he surprisingly observed about 587 lines in the spectrum of the sun. The observation was quite puzzling! The 'black line puzzle' was later resolved by Bunsen and Kirchoff. They interpreted them as 'elemental signatures' that helped in understanding not only the structure of atom but also of the stellar constitution. Thus we see that Fraunhofer's contributions were most fundamental in nature that paved the way to understand matter at deeper level.

Fraunhofer's great devotion for his glass work earned him honorary doctorate and award of merit. A class of diffraction is known after his name. It's a rare example in the history of science that tells us how a poor orphan could develop himself into a highly skilled craftsman and physicist in true sense. It inspires and touches our heart.

Michael Faraday

The path created by Faraday is highly motivating and inspiring. Coming from a very poor blacksmith's family Faraday, without having any formal education, forged himself into a true scientist. He was the greatest of great experimental physicists of his time who applied his intellectual gifts in studying electricity and magnetism, and finally succeeded in getting 'electricity' from 'magnetism'. He actually discovered a new phenomenon 'electromagnetism'. When he started his researches, electricity and magnetism were considered to be of no any practical value. It was the period, when physics was becoming more and more mathematical but he produced research papers that contained no mathematics. Actually, it was his inner interest in science that ultimately made him the 'father of modern physics'.

If we look at Faraday's life, we find many inspiring moments. His family could not afford even his schooling and he received very little formal education. At the age of 14, he was to join an apprenticeship to help his family. But it was here; he got an opportunity to read many books and decided to enter in the world of science. The books not only trained his mind to be an excellent experimentalist but also helped him in choosing the field of electricity to work in. Isaac Watt's book 'The Improvement of Mind' and Jane Marcet's book 'Conversation of Chemistry' had lasting influence on him. But he didn't know the way how to enter in the field of science. He got one way out. As he was acquainted with Davy, he started attending Davy's public lecture. Now he decided to approach Davy. For this, he prepared notes of Davy's public lecture and sent the bound volume to him. Davy got impressed and appreciated his zealous interest, fine memory and great attentiveness. After few months, he gave a chance to him. Happy Faraday, thus, joined Davy and started learning the basics of science.

Faraday soon got an opportunity to accompany Davy, as an assistant in a lecture trip. During this trip, he got not only the access to the scientific circle of Europe but also got so many stimulating seed ideas to work on. Soon, he got freedom to pursue as independent scientific worker and so started working out the ideas. He never looked back and made many revolutionary contributions.

Faraday is a great source of inspiration and a rare example, which showed that the quality work can be done even under odd circumstances by remaining curious, cool, composed and committed.

Milton A. Humason

Like Faraday, Humason also had no initial training but succeeded in forging himself into a great astronomer of the twentieth century. His story inspires many. According to his biography, he took a year off from the school. When 14, he planned to stay on the site of Mount Wilson and find work. Here, he worked as a mule driver. It was during this period, 'Mount Wilson Observatory' project began. He took material and equipment to the observatory site and started observing curiously the way scientists were working. Out of sheer interest once, he volunteered to be a night assistant and this proved a turning point for him to become an astronomer. It was because of his unusual ability as an observer and had great patience, skill and diligence. George Ellery Hale, the project leader, noticed these qualities and appointed him to his scientific staff, where he joined Edwin Hubble in a project. Humason painstakingly measured the spectra of more than 550 galaxies and provided evidence of 'red shift'. 'Red shift' means, all galaxies are moving away from earth. This gave a new picture of 'expanding universe'. The credit of much of the Hubble's success goes to Humason. Actually, his ability to handle the instruments with great care and to work with them patiently and skillfully was unbeatable.

Humason life inspires and motivated to take risk and convert opportunity into an advantage.

Meghnad Saha

Meghnad Saha's biography is highly inspiring. It tells us about the way a grocer's son became world class scientist. Meghnad's father, a poor businessman, wanted his son to start earning after the completion of his primary schooling. But his teachers, who were highly impressed by his brilliance and talent, didn't want so. They approached his father and got him convinced. So, his further education continued in a nearby village but for higher education, he was to shift to Calcutta (Kolkata). He shifted and joined Presidency college but without any financial support from his helpless father. In Kolkata, he was to earn on his own to stay and study. These were truly difficult days, but determined Meghnad never lost confidence. He worked hard, gave home tuitions to the students but never left his own studies.

Meghnad was happy to find academic and inspiring environment in the college. This helped him in molding his thinking. He had teachers like P.C. Ray and J.C. Bose to get inspiration and classmates like P.C. Mahalanobis and S.N. Bose to discuss. Letter, with Satyendra Nath Bose, he translated Einstein's theory of relativity in English. He tried to remain in touch with the frontier of science. It is in this course, he came to know about a puzzling result related to the origin of a mysterious spectral line in the upper part of chromo-sphere of sun. He solved the puzzle and discovered a formula, now known after his name. This formula is so fundamental in nature that nearly all later research and progress in astrophysics is influenced by it. He became a 'tall and inspirational figure' in the astrophysical world. His ideas and opinions were highly influential. His simplicity, un-mindfulness of personal comforts, untiring energy and dedication for his work are the real sources of inspirations for us.

Antoine Henri Becquerel

Becquerel came from a family of scientific traditions. His great-grandfather, grandfather and father were also scientists. Keeping interest alive in science for four generations is rare. Becquerel's level of confidence was very high. His power of attention was supreme. His way of analysis was very logical and methodical. These are some of his qualities that inspire us.

According to his biography, initially he was interested in studying the emission of visible light from the UV-exposed materials. For detailed studies, he collected some minerals and placed them in the drawer of his table in which he used to keep all-important things including photographic plates.

One day, he came to know that the sealed photographic plates in the drawer had got damaged. The reason was unknown. He got puzzled. He repeated the experiment and got convinced that he had discovered a new phenomenon. His materials could quite spontaneously produce radiation without any external supply of energy. But this surprised him. How could it be possible? Logically, he thought of some source to be present in the mineral itself. But what is that inexhaustible source? It remained mystery for quite some years till Ernest Rutherford came with his research on the structure of atom. The answer was hidden in the atomic nucleus. The confidence of Becquerel is really admirable. It proves that if our observations are foolproof, we should not hesitate in proposing new idea even if it goes against the prevailing belief and common sense.

Madam Marry Curie

Madam Curie has created history as two-time winner of Nobel Prize. She got fascinated by Becquerel's discovery of radioactivity and decided to work with her husband Pierre. From Becquerel they learnt that even after extracting uranium from pitch blend, the material is showing radioactivity. This prompted Curies to create the chemical kitchen in the store of the School of Physics in Paris. Marie concentrated on the chemical side of the problem whereas her husband Pierre concentrated on the physics side. A truly coordinated effort! In the chemical kitchen, they worked with untiring energy and zeal round the clock. Finally, they succeeded in discovering new radioactive elements as per expectations. This unique 'husband-wife' team won the Nobel Prize for physics in 1903 along with Henry Becquerel. Unfortunately,

Pierre died in a road accident in 1906. When News came to her, she was teaching in the class. But she continued and finished the class. It is inspiring to learn that even her husband's death did not stop her in completing her duties. She continued teaching till the class was over. After the death of her husband, she carried forward the mission. She continued the unfinished work and succeeded in winning another 'Nobel Prize' but for chemistry this time, in 1911.

Madam Curie proved that interest and commitment can lead us anywhere. She inspired many. No one can teach better than Madam Curie as how to face hardship and continue scientific journey under adverse conditions.

Ernest Rutherford

Rutherford is a rare scientist and leading explorer of the vast and complex universe within atom. It is his genius that discovered such mysteries that radically altered our understanding of Nature. His way of solving any problem used to be simple and straight forward. His intuitive power was supreme. After the discovery of proton, his prediction about the existence of 'neutron' in nucleus surprises even today.

Rutherford's biography inspires a lot. He is a unique example who created pathways from a rural child to the most illustrious scientist. His being a voracious reader helped him in impressing his school teachers. As a scientist, he contributed in the areas of physics and chemistry. But these were not the subjects taught in rural schools of his country, New Zealand in those days. So, it is quite fascinating to know his epoch making journey. In his early school days, he influenced his teachers by his great interest in literature and mathematics. But Rutherford was silently getting attracted towards a young teacher W.S. Little John. He used to tell him about the excitements and wonders of physics that were taking place in Europe. His interest continued growing but it was only when he got an opportunity to work in Cambridge, his real talent got crystallized. He was impressed by J.J. Thomson, who while studying cathode rays discovered electron, a minute particles as constituent of matter and proposed first 'water melon like atom model'. Rutherford discovered a nucleus and proposed a new 'solar system like atom model' discarding that of Thomson. His alpha-particle scattering experiment is considered as one of the greatest experiment of physics. Atomic pioneer Neils Bohr took a lot of inspiration from him.

Enrico Fermi

Fermi is one of the giants of the twentieth century world of physics. His contributions were enormous and highly influential. He always remained at the forefront of activities and was involved in many breakthroughs in physics. Like S.N. Bose and Albert Einstein, Fermi collaborated with P.A.M. Dirac in discovering a statistics, now known as Fermi-Dirac statistics. It deals with a category of particles known after his name as 'Fermions'. At that time, intense research activities were going on in the field of radioactivity. After explanation of alpha decay in terms of 'quantum tunneling', it was now the turn of beta decay. Its spectrum was quite puzzling. Pauli speculated the emission of 'neutrino' along with beta decay. But the decay process of neutron was not clear. It was Fermi who developed a theory quite brilliantly and innovatively. In his theory, he did not assume decay products to be present in the neutron before decay. He compared the situation with photon emission from atom. We know that the emitted photon is not present in the atom but is created during the electronic transition. He thought likewise. By considering neutron and proton as two states of a single particle 'nucleon', beta emission can be achieved in terms of nucleonic transition.

Fermi got impressed by the discovery of 'artificial radioactivity' by Irène Curie and her husband Frederic. Fermi thought of inducing artificial radioactivity by using neutrons of varying speeds. He succeeded in discovering many new radioisotopes. During this investigation, he found that the 'slow neutrons' are more effective than alpha particles. With uranium, he obtained some puzzling results. Otto Hahn, Lise Meitner and Fritz Strassmann had repeated Fermi's experiments and discovered 'nuclear fission'. This work, thus, opened a new way of harnessing energy from atom.

Fermi tackled wide-ranging problems and today, since the learning of physics starts with matter, 'he' as 'fermion' is present all over the material world. It is hard to imagine any discussion in physics without Fermion and Fermi! He was a very clear thinker, dedicated physicist and great team leader. He excelled in experimental as well as theoretical fields and was outstanding in both. He continues to live in our hearts as the chief architect of the nuclear age.

George Gamow

Gamow is known as a man with wide-ranging interest not only in the nucleus of the atom and living cell but also in the cosmos in the history of science. His biography tells that 'astronomical telescope', a birthday gift from his father, proved to be a great motivator for him. He used that gifted 'toy' as a tool to explore the sky with great patience in nights. While observing twinkling stars, Gamow, the curious boy, decided to become a scientist.

Gamow didn't take much time in realizing the potential of the then newly born 'quantum mechanics' and the probabilistic interpretation of quantum mechanical states. He thoroughly studied the works of quantum scientists Schrödinger, Heisenberg, Dirac, Born and others. Gamow being quite imaginative and free from any bias, soon applied quantum mechanical concepts and solved the then mysterious problem of alpha decay. It is here, he discovered 'tunneling effect'.

He showed creative interest in science all through his life. He always bubbled with innovative ideas. His contributions in various astrophysical areas like star formation and stellar nucleosynthesis, After Hubble's discovery of expanding universe, when Big Bang theory of universe is proposed, his work provided strong theoretical support to it. He applied thermodynamic concepts to make predictions about 'cosmic microwave background radiation' (CMBR), which were later discovered by Arno Penzias and Robert Wilson.

Gamow discovered a lot, conjectured much and shared his sense of wonder with all of us through his stylish writings. His unique style of writing popular science made him very special. His writings have profound influence and inspiration. Truly, Gamow and his enormous contributions will remain as everlasting source of inspiration for young students, teachers and scientists.

Stephen Hawking

Hawking is one of the great minds of the twentieth century. He is known today for his ground-breaking work in physics and cosmology. He authored exciting popular science books like 'A Brief History of Time', 'The Universe in a Nutshell' and 'The Grand Design'.

Because of Amyotrophic Lateral Sclerosis disease none of the parts of Hawking's body, other than his mind, is under his control. Doctors considered it as a 'gone case' and gave him two and a half years to live when he was 21 and still a student. He ignored what doctor said about him and concentrated deeply on astrophysical research and finally proved them wrong. His contributions on 'black hole' made him a world's leading cosmologist. He showed theoretically that even black holes can leak information. He demonstrated that it emits radiation (known as Hawking Radiation). The radiation is made of material particles. It is amazing that matter can escape the enormous gravitational field! Thus, his theory brought a conceptual change in the very understanding of black holes.

He proved that if aim is high and determination and dedication perfect, death cannot touch a person. He has crossed 72 and still continuing creative works.... Who can be a better inspirer than him?

C. V. Raman

Raman was highly inquisitive, ambitious and hardworking. He was a true teacher, a seeker of truth and a man of supreme confidence. Science had a deep impression on his mind. He never limited himself to narrow sphere. He tackled variety of problems and did research on sound, light, rocks, flowers, atmosphere and weather and also on physiology of vision and hearing. He was a prolific researcher and writer of scientific books. Raman inculcated reading habits from very childhood. The light of Asia, The Elements of Euclid, The Sensation of Tone, The Physiology of Vision and Lord Rayleigh's Collected Papers influenced him a lot. He was a keen and careful observer. At 16, he got his first paper published in Philosophical Magazine of London. He was inspired by the works of Helmholtz and Lord Rayleigh and became a source of inspiration to many.

His love for science remained alive even while remaining in the job of Assistant Accountant General. He started working on part-time basis in Indian Association for Cultivation of Science. He used to question facts of Nature. During a sea voyage to England, he was attracted by the deep blue colour of the sea. His asked himself 'why could it not be a case of light being scattered by water molecules just like air molecules in atmosphere'. He used to keep a pocket spectrometer with him. He conducted experiment on the deck itself and got some favourable preliminary results. He decided to work on the problem very seriously. The efforts put by him culminated into what is today known as 'Raman Effect'. Raman offered quantum mechanical explanation for his effect. When he demonstrated the involvement of molecular vibration and rotation, it became a very sensitive tool to study the internal structures of molecules.

His boundless curiosity, spirit of enquiry and devotion inspired many and will continue to inspire young minds in future.

S. Chandrasekhar

`Chandrasekhar was a great astrophysicist. He dedicated his life to the pursuit of science. 'Forever learning' was the motivation for him in pursuing science. The book on 'The Internal Constitution of Stars' by A. Eddington and another on 'Atomic Structure and Spectral Lines' by A. Sommerfeld in his college days inspired and helped him to choose astrophysics as his career. He is famous for his revolutionary work on the theory of stars. Working on science used to give him serenity and inner peace.

After completing education in India, Chandrasekhar got an opportunity to do research in England. Like Raman, he too got an idea to understand the life of stars, while on sea voyage. In the stars, a tug of war - like situation exists. This emerges because of the presence of inward gravitational pull and the outward radiation push. The equilibrium persists for quite long period but when star's fuel gets exhausted, gravitation temporarily wins and star starts contracting. The contraction stops when stellar matter transforms into 'neutrons' and quantum mechanics takes the control to stop gravitational influence. A new equilibrium is established. He employed quantum mechanical concepts and predicted the fate of a star when all its remaining fuel gets exhausted.

He succeeded in discovering nature's secret in terms of the mass- limit (known as Chandrasekhar limit) that decides the ultimate fate of the dying star. In very massive stars, gravitation finally wins resulting into 'black holes'.

Chandrasekhar's life is a unique example that proved that we can achieve great heights through strong will power, thorough understanding, self-confidence and patience.

'Non-physicist' physicists in the world of physics

Reading history inspires and creates interest. It teaches how to face trying moments that we come across in life. It is astonishing to learn from history that the world of physics has not only attracted the professional physicists but also those who had initial academic career and work in other fields. These areas include Law (Avogadro, who is famous for a number, known after his name, Avogadro number), Law and Economics (James Franck, who is famous for Franck-Hertz Experiment and who won Nobel with Hertz in 1925), Pharmacy (Hans Christian Oersted, who is famous for discovering the magnetic effect of electric current which he discovered and is known after his name), Medical (Thomas Young, famous for his work on interference of light which established the wave nature of light and Hermann Helmholtz, who extended the principle of conservation of energy to include all forms of energy), Chemistry (Isidor Isaac Rabi, who won 1944's Nobel for his development of the resonance method to measure electronic dipole moment which later proved to be a key step in the development of Quantum Electrodynamics; Louis Walter Alvareg, who won 1968's Nobel for developing particle accelerator; Michael Faraday, who is the father of modern physics and famous for producing electricity from magnetism), Chemical Engineering (Eugene Paul Wigner, who won 1963's Nobel for his work on the law of conservation of parity in nuclear reactions; Martin Lewis Perl, who won 1995's Nobel for the discovery of tau lepton), Electrical Engineering (Henry Becquerel, who won 1903's Nobel for the discovery of radioactivity; Piotr Keonidovich Kapitsa (or Peter Kapitza), who won 1978's Nobel for his contributions to the understanding of the low-temperature physics; Heinrich George Barkhausen, who is famous for the effect that he discovered in ferromagnetic materials which proved the existence of domains and also for evolving a criterion to make an electronic circuit oscillating; Peter Joseph William Debye, who won 1936's Nobel for his work on structure of molecules; Paul Dirac who won 1933's Nobel for the development of Quantum Mechanics; John Bardeen, who won his 1956's Nobel for the discovery of transistor and another 1972's Nobel for the BCS theory of superconductors), Mechanical Engineering (Ivar Giaever, who won 1973's Nobel for his work on superconducting junction; Homi Jahangir Bhabha, who is known for his cascade theory in cosmic rays and Bhabha scattering), Civil Engineering (Fresnel, who is famous for his pioneering work on diffraction and polarization of light), Business and Engineering (Lebedev, who is famous for the measurement of radiation pressure), Mathematics (Doppler, who is famous for the discovery of Doppler effect; John Douglas Cockcroft, who won 1951's Nobel for his work on nuclear reactions which proved that protons could tunnel into target nuclei at much lower energy; Marya Goeppert Mayer, who won 1963's Nobel for her work on nuclear shell model), History (de Broglie, who is famous for his matter wave hypothesis).

From the above list, we come to know that many scientists joined physics after having studied the subjects closer to physics like chemistry, biology, pharmacy, medical or engineering. But finding the names of the persons having History, Law, Economics, Business and other subjects as their background, surprises us. Further, the above list also includes the names of persons who had not even formal education to undertake research as career and also those who lived a life of hardships. Some of the great physicists like Einstein were certified by their teachers as dull and mentally retarded. What does this indicate? It is the interest and the intense desire that counts. Where there is will, there is way. The family background, initial academic background, subject knowledge, primary training, facilities etc. matter little.

One more thing worth mentioning is about the very nature of physics. It expresses itself in different languages. When we come across 'principle of least action' and 'least time', we find physics talking in the language of 'economics'. But dynamic nature of thermal and mechanical systems along with the knowledge of unachievable 100% 'efficiency' attract economist and market people involved in 'planning'. The crystallography that deals with symmetries and patterns take us in the world of 'arts' and 'paintings'. Acoustics takes us in the world of 'music'. The radioactivity and natural clocks take us in the evolutionary phase of earth and also in the 'history of culture'. Further, while studying plasmas and condensed matter, we come across 'collective behaviour' of the system that reminds us of our social behaviour. The inferences on relationships and interdependence drawn from newly emerged 'particle physics' takes us closer to sociology, where holistic and ecological approaches play key roles. The quantum field theoretical views provide a possibility of reaching in the 'spiritual world'. The relativity and quantum mechanics takes us in the mystic wonderland reminding mythology.

In this way, we see physics to be a wonderful area of activity in science. It extends help and provides solution to almost all problems. Many undercurrents can be experienced while studying physics. These are related to 'technology' and 'education'. In past centuries, we have successfully tapped the 'technology' to change the outer world that we live in. But the feeling of happiness and security are far from us. It is because of our failure to discover the educational resources which are inherently present in the scientific concepts. Now the time has come to discover and to tap them.

8

PHYSICS AND EDUCATION: MESSAGES

Physics has a wonderful range, on one end it talks to philosophy on the hazy limits of our knowledge about "the cause" and "the purpose" or "the gamble of dice---chance" and "the Grand Design" or "the fundamental" and "the emergent" while on the other end it determines the fate of technology in a really very concrete way widening the ability of humankind that may one day match the persona of the imagined 'God'. It is said that technology appeared much before the conceptual understanding of physics in the remote past. That was but the work of intuition--- the naïve sparks of human genius, nevertheless the true technology began only after the rationalization of intuitive curiosities of the human mind about the world that formed the fundamentals of physics.

The study of physics provides inroads practically in all disciplines of sciences like chemistry, biology etc. and is continuously providing us the 'resource points' that may be tapped. Some of them have wishfully been exploited by technologists in order to create a technological world around us. The tremendous growth in the areas like energy, communication, transportation, industry, environment, medicine, meteorology, defense etc. that we see today would have not been possible without physics. With this point of view, physics may be called as a 'technology booster' that we come across in a relationship between 'science and technology'.

It may be said about Physics or science as a whole that it has nothing in its structural concreteness or in its underlying abstractness which leads us to realize that the principles of physical design command for a moral life. Of course, it may be meekly truer for technology but not quite so for Physics or science in general. Science cannot accommodate lies and it has always upheld the flag of Truth at every event of such struggles in the history. It shows highest morality with respect to the truth. In every respect the laws of physics can inspire us to live in coexistence, coordination and integration. On the basis of our experiences and visiting physics that has grown so far, we can say that physics is a human creative intellectual activity like art and music. All great experiments in physics may truly be seen as a work of fine arts. The applications of physics help in forging and enriching our cultural experiences.

Interestingly, twentieth century physics that penetrated atom has changed its direction and approach. Bohr's statement 'when it comes to atom, the language can be used only as poetry' tells a lot about the spirit of physics. Poetry is very close to human emotions and feelings. Further, physics looks apparently mathematical but it is not so. Mathematics is a tool of physics. Stripped of mathematics, physics becomes pure enchantment'. This can be experienced while going through relativity physics, quantum physics and particle physics. Actually, physics wonders at the way things are and a divine interest in how that is so. For this physics discovers new relationships and finds new connections. The connections between mechanics and acoustics, mechanics and heat, electricity and magnetism, electromagnetism and optics, mechanics and electromagnetism, electromagnetism and weak nuclear force etc. are well known. The discovery of relationships between space and time or between mass and energy have changed the very direction of physics. We find universal joy in making new connections. So, relationships are precious and important not only in physics but in life also. While studying physics, we come across many hidden and unexplored relationships that are very close to human psyche and behaviour. They may be termed as 'life-building resource points'. If we are able to discover them, we find a new relationship between 'physics and education'. The knowledge of this fills us with value-consciousness, where wisdom gets awaken while applying physics. Their knowledge may help us in number of ways in shaping our life. Let us see some of the educational resource points which are inherently present in the stream of physics.

1. Problems in physics are related to various physical situations. So, the efforts required to solve the problems plays major indirect role in carving out the personality of the person involved. It helps in inducing rational thinking, youthful enthusiasm, self-control, inexhaustible curiosity, self-discipline and boldness, all basic ingredients necessary for undertaking any creative pursuit. Thus, we see that physics makes us strong to live happily and guides us in making the earth a beautiful place to live.

2. While solving physical problems, we realize the importance of 'initial conditions'. The study of chaotic systems shows that these systems are greatly affected and apparently grow quite different by their initial state. It demonstrates that a small change in the initial conditions of apparently looking similar systems may grow quite differently and we observe large differences at a later stage. The observation of 'butterfly effect' while studying the 'chaotic systems' like atmosphere is a good example. In our life also initial conditions, in which we born and grow, are important. We may grow quite differently even if we belong to same family. So, it is necessary to pay much attention on the initial conditions during our habit building age. This will decide how we will grow and become in future.

3. While handling problems, we come across 'frame of references', 'coordinate systems', 'projections' etc. Coordinate systems used in physics provide different ways of describing the system in question. Working with one type of system may provide a 'solution but not the ease'. For a sphere, the 'spherical polar coordinate system' is proper and not the 'Cartesian coordinate system'. So, its proper selection is important. We need to consider various options available and select the suitable one. In absence of suitable option, we need to be innovative while solving realistic problems in life too. The importance of frame of reference may be realized with otherwise unconceivable conclusions after the discovery of theory of relativity. The relative nature of observations creates puzzling situations. Only a thorough understanding of the frame wherefrom the event is observed by different observers, helps in

resolving the puzzle. Actually, knowledge and use of frame of references help in thinking critically and creatively about an event observed by different observers in different ways and in settling many puzzling issues. We come across many complicated situations in our daily life too. And, it becomes the reason of conflicts and debate at number of occasions. Truly, the conflicts are inevitable when we live in a society, but by looking at events with others frame and giving room to other's viewpoints will surely help in resolving the conflict. There are many projections of one reality. This depends on the way one observes. So, each projection becomes individual's reality. Mathematics provides a way to formulate the reality and all solutions are present there. The conditions are prescribed for one particular solution that can be realized. They actually provide us different facets of the same reality. A three dimensional body like cylinder or sphere can give its projection as circle in two dimensions. So, by seeing the projections, we cannot be sure about the shape of real objects. Similarly, different projections may be observed of the same reality. Say, for example we may have rectangle or circle as projections of a cylindrical body. That's why, what we observe is actually a 'relative reality'. Each reality is observer-dependent and creation of observer's own knowledge base, measuring skills and ability of his senses. It is worth remembering here that the experiences of color-blind or tone-deaf persons are different than normal persons. Thus, the study of 'Projections' in physics guide us to accommodate different viewpoints while resolving puzzling situations in our life. When we draw conclusions based on our realized potential, we may be right but others may not be wrong because our truths may not necessarily be the truths of others.

4. While studying physics, we come across the concepts of displacement, inertia, force, torque etc. For moving forward, force is required and not the torque. Torque produces rotational motion. While studying rotational systems, we see that axial points always remain static. This makes us realize that there are also safe places in the dynamic world where we can work peacefully. The effect of changing momentum and magnetic flux is well known in physics. The one generates the mechanical force while the other electromotive force. Nothing 'new' appears when they remain constant. It is an important educational resource point, which tells us that monotony can't yield creative pleasures. We need to break 'inertia'. Newton's law of action and reaction, and Lenz's law have lot to say about human nature and psyche. The principle of least action is also worth remembering. It depicts human nature and tendency. This principle tells that the path may be of any length but action should be least. The amount of action however cannot be zero. This inference is drawn from quantum physics.

5. Matter exists in different states. It is the environment that brings the matter in a particular state. The liquid water may exist in the form of ice or steam. So, the state may be altered by changing the environment. Millions of collisions are taking place between gas molecules at NTP (Normal Temperature and Pressure). So, microscopically the molecules in a gas are in chaotic state. But macroscopically some such characteristic properties emerge in the gas which gives rise to gas laws.

In liquid also we see the chaotic behavior when we heat it. But soon we see convection currents start developing. In other words, we see creation of 'order'. The message is clear that the creative opportunities are there even in most unfavourable conditions.

6. The study of the behaviour of the material at low temperature is worth noting. At low temperatures, molecular binding results into liquid and solid states. Further, we also know that there are some conditions that may keep water as liquid even below zero degree Celsius. We can learn a lesson from here that even under adverse conditions one can survive and maintain its identity.

7. The effect of ultra-low cooling is observed in the emergence of miraculous property 'superconductivity' in some materials. BCS theory has been proposed to explain it. It tells that at ultra-low temperature, the electrons form 'cooper pairs' which give birth to the phenomenon of superconductivity. At high temperature, the pairs are not formed and so freely moving electrons collide with phonons (quantum of lattice vibrational energy) and give rise to resistance. At low resistance, the phonon helps in forming the electron pairs. So this activity of pair formation highlights the effect of remaining cool. It tells us that by remaining cool, we can make even our enemies as our friends.

8. Physicists explain the phenomena like viscosity, surface tension, elasticity etc. using molecular theories. The study of viscous force is very important in hydrodynamics. The upper layer moves faster than the lower in the fluids. A

momentum transfer takes place between neighbouring fluid layers so as to move together. We can take this as an advice to live in a family. In order to live and move together and also to avoid conflicts, older generations need to move faster and the new generations a bit slower.

9. In a liquid, we see 'tension' at the surface but no tension inside. However, the molecules are not at rest there. They move randomly inside. This gives us a very good lesson that it is not possible to avoid tension in our busy life but we can manage it. Let the tension remain at the surface. We should not allow it to enter into our mind.

10. The study of 'conductor' and 'current carrying conductor' is very important. Both the conductors are identical with material point of view but there is enormous difference between them. The electrons are in motion in both the cases. But electrons move randomly with no sense of direction in one case while they move in guided manner in the other. This makes them different. Physics thus guides us to create internal currents to be creative and different than others.

11. While studying thermodynamics, we come across thermodynamic laws. These are the basic laws of physics. According to them, it is logical to say that 'perpetual motion machines' of any kind are impossible to make. The efficiency of any machine cannot be 100% percent. We need to put efforts as no free lunch or dinner is available in Nature.

12. While studying different types of waves, we come across ups and downs, rise and fall. But with every fall, there is

a rise in a wave. It describes the life situations and tells us not to worry at the time of fall. A rise is bound to come. At the same time, it is giving a warning message also, not to have proud, when we are on rise.

13. The phenomena like echo, resonance, interference, diffraction, polarization etc. are quite rich as educational resource points. We come across reflection, refraction, total internal reflection while studying optical properties of material. Many natural events like rainbow, mirage etc. are explained by understanding the propagation of light while crossing different media boundaries. Mirage creates illusion by creating false image of a water body at observer's location. The observer logically interprets it as a reality, which is not actually there. The illusions occur in real life also. The knowledge of the phenomenon of mirage may be taken as a warning. It tells us that what we are seeing may not be a reality. We come across this type of situation while studying fields. Electrostatic field due to charged conducting sphere at different points outside the sphere suggests that the charge is concentrated at the centre. But when we choose a point inside the sphere, we find no charge is actually present at the centre. In life also, we face similar situations many times and with partial knowledge, we pass our life believing in our experienced reality. We should realize that the things may not exist, even if they appear to exist.

14. We know that a stretched string can vibrate in different modes. Fundamental frequency of a vibrating string changes by changing the tension. So, by changing the environment and conditions, we can create other

possibilities in life. At very high temperature, matter exists in its fourth state, called plasma. Plasma sustains infinite number of modes of vibration. We are familiar with another situation where different harmonics may be produced in air columns and modes may be excited in stretched string. Only those modes may be excited which are potentially present in the system. This reminds us that what we can become is always potentially present within us. We need to know and strive hard to become.

15. With electrical conduction point of view, matter can be classified as conductors, insulators and semiconductors. Effect of doping in semiconductors is widely studied in physics. It suggests that great effects may be observed by making small but appropriate changes. This gives us an inspirational message that even if we are one in million or billon, we can bring effective changes.

16. The atoms and molecules and their characteristic properties also have a lot to say. While studying structure of atom, we notice that addition of one proton changes inert neon into active sodium. This gives us a message that one positive change is enough to bring the change in our personality. In molecules, atoms form bonds. Here, they get associated but maintain the identity. The molecules exhibit the properties, which were not present in individual atoms forming them. The properties of hydrogen and oxygen are not found in water. In life also, the magic of proper association may emerge while working on a project.

17. The atoms and molecules are quantum objects. They are found in different discrete energy states. In the

normal state, they reside in minimum energy state. But on getting energy from some external source, they get excited and occupy one of the excited state. Their life time in the excited state is very small. They soon return to the ground state. A lot of learning is inherently present here. If we get excited, we should return to normal state soon.

18. Fluorescence is a well-known phenomenon. Fluorescent materials find various applications. Roadside milestones are coated with these materials, so that they become visible in dark nights but only if we have light to throw on them. The message is clear that guidance will be available if we have light in form of curiosity.

19. The atoms are made of charged entities like electrons and protons, which make them tiny magnets. These are randomly distributed in the material. Some materials like iron are ferromagnetic in nature which can be used to build permanent magnets. This is done by rubbing a permanent magnet over the bar of iron along the length again and again but in the same direction. This rubbing process helps in bringing orderliness by orienting the tiny (atomic) magnets present and randomly distributed in the bar. This highlights the importance of orientation in professional and social life. The orientation can make us special and different.

20. The study of the behavior of protons in and outside nucleus also has a lot to say. We know that the protons repel outside the nucleus but when forced to confine in a limited nuclear space, they keep aside their 'charge' which repel them and change the 'terms' to remain

together. A great lesson for us that there may be some points of aversion, but conditions are always there to come together and work.

21. While studying properties of nucleus, we come across natural and artificial radioactivity, alpha decay, fission, fusion etc. These are potential resource points with education point of view. The radioactive alpha decay is explained by 'tunneling effect'. It is a quantum effect. In this effect a particle with less energy can tunnel through a potential barrier. This shows that a classically impossible event is quantum mechanically possible. This suggests us to believe that nothing is impossible. Alternatives are always there. From artificial radioactivity, we can learn that it is possible to bring such changes in life which can make us self-inspiring person. Nuclear fusion tells us that, if we want to live together, we need to sacrifice. Nuclear fission gives a message that a quarrel in the crowd is inevitable and is a potential cause of disintegration. From this educational resource point we learn that crowds should be avoided for developing sustainable family or society. This suggests the need to go for population control.

22. While studying quantum systems, we come across uncertainty principle, which is a guiding principle for the quantum world. Uncertainty ensures creativity. Heisenberg's uncertainty principle tells us that nothing is impossible. A path is always there. Heisenberg once said that what we observe is not Nature itself but Nature exposed to our methods of questioning. According to this principle, we cannot determine energy and time precisely. Therefore, it is possible for a group of particles

with non-zero total energy to be created out of nothing and then disappear within a short time. More energy may be available but for shorter periods for the purpose. Annihilation and creation of virtual field quanta in vacuum take place continuously. This gives rise to **quantum fluctuations** which shows that the vacuum cannot be characterized by the presence of 'nothing'. In life also, there cannot be a state of nothingness even if we lose everything. Hope is always there.

23. Up to nuclear level, the forces are relatively weak and relativistic effects exists but do not dominate. So, it's a good approximately to say that the things are made of constituents. But below nuclear level, the way of seeing things change. While studying particle physics, we learn about the behavior of the subatomic and elementary particles. Here, matter is always associated with a field that cannot be separated from it. The particle world is governed by Einstein's relativity and uncertainty principle. Because of these, every particle continuously involves in the process of creation and annihilation. This implies that matter cannot be separated from its activities and it continues involving in self-interaction. So, the interaction of the particle decides its properties. The classical notion of composite objects consisting of a definite set of constituent parts does not work here. Two energetic protons may break up into a great variety of fragments after interaction. It depends on energy involved. Here, dynamic energy, patterns are dissolved and rearranged and the static concepts of composite objects and constituent parts cannot be applied to these patterns. So, the particles have no meaning as isolated entity and can only be seen as integrated part of the

whole. At elementary particle level, we notice a shift from object to relationship. Physics tells us that the system is integrated whole whose essential properties emerge from the relationships between the parts. A great lesson with ecological point of view.

24. Astrophysical studies also have to say much. Big bang theory of universe is most respected theory. It says that about 13 billion years ago, there was a 'point universe'. It was perfectly symmetric. After big bang, with the passage of time, symmetry started breaking and diversities started appearing. Thus, all our today's apparent diversities have common origin. This suggests us that we are inherently connected with each other.

In the above description, we have seen some of the resource points with education point of view. There may be many more such points that may be discovered. Our efforts in this direction are important as 'technology' has been tapped from science that has helped us in growing externally. Now, the time has come to tap the 'education' from the flow of science to grow internally. In the following section, we are going to see some messages that can be drawn while studying physics.

Stress/tension is essential for creativity

We come across the term 'tension or stress' at various occasions while studying physics. We know that the vibrational modes are produced in stretched strings or membranes. For stretching 'tension' is applied. In many electrical circuits we employ condensers (capacitors). The stress exists between the charged plates of condenser. But there is a limit to bear the stress. This stress is 'system specific' property. If one breaks the limit, (dielectric) breakdown occurs and condenser gets burnt. Similarly, while studying 'elasticity', we come across 'fatigue effect' that appears in 'stressed mechanical systems'. This causes the weakening of the material when we repeatedly load and unload or apply a load for a longer period of time. This causes progressive and localized structural damages of temporary or permanent nature. Thus, physics gives us a message that we are required to have tension to be creative but we should never exceed the limit and remain in over-stressed condition as it is dangerous. We should always keep in mind about our potential and stress bearing capability.

Conflicts are inevitable but can be resolved

We are familiar with three-dimensional world but after the discovery of theory of relativity, the picture changed. Think of matter and energy. They require minimum three dimensions for their meaningful expression. They look two different physical entities in three-dimensional world. They look opposite to each other. But in four-dimensional space-time world, they become equivalent. Thus, the opposite and seemingly conflicting behaviour is an indication that we are in the world of lower dimensions. If we move to higher dimensions, the differences vanish. Similarly, think of a 'simple pendulum'. It executes 'simple harmonic motion' (to and fro periodic motion). The bob of the pendulum oscillates between two extremes, opposite to each other. This is simple motion in one-dimensional world, for small oscillations. If this simple harmonic motion is expressed in 'two-dimensional world', then it becomes circular motion having no extremes. Thus, the differences that appear in 'lower-dimensional world' disappear in the 'higher-dimensional world'. From here, we get a message that the apparent differences, oppositeness and conflicts that we see in the society are because of our living in lower dimensional mental world. These will vanish, when we move to higher dimensions. Thus to make the conflict-free world, we should give up narrow-mindedness.

Tolerance

After the discovery of quantum mechanics and theory of relativity, the foundation of physics has changed. The frame of reference and experimental conditions have become very important. The 'uncertainty' and 'indeterminacy' have qualified to find places in the language of physics. They have positive values like flexibility, open-mindedness, and tolerance. While describing a quantum system, we use the wave function. The wave function is completely defined only if it accommodates all possible experimentally observable states. Thus, all viewpoints are important with the point of view of physics. 'An individual is correct' doesn't now mean that all the remaining others are wrong. Physics tells us to remember that a thing or event might look quite different upon changing the frame of reference. Thus, physics gives a clear message that we should be free from all biases. The need of the hour for us to be tolerant and refrain from quarrelling over trifling matters.

We see only, what we want to see

The language of physics for the micro-world has become very powerful through its metaphoric and hypothetical nature. Every metaphor and symbol e.g. ψ, can be used to describe our experiences in the world. But our experiences are based only on the limited aspects that we choose to observe. Thus, the meaning associated with the symbol is valid in a particular context only. According to the theory of relativity, the time measurement of one person may not coincide with that of the other. Further, even the causality and simultaneity have lost their meanings and have become relative and subjective quantities. Thus, for any observation, 'subject' or 'observer' is important, as it is a part of the experimental system. According to physics, the light has a dual nature, i.e. wave nature or particle nature. Both of these properties are complementary and so cannot be observed by performing one experiment. If we want to see wave nature of light, we have to perform an experiment demonstrating interference or diffraction. But to see its particle nature, we are to perform an experiment demonstrating photoelectric effect. In other words, we actually see what we want to see. Thus, the message from physics is to look for all the good that exists in the surroundings. This will make us positive, optimistic and useful for the society.

Allow creative persons to work without disturbing them

The double slit experiment of Thomas Young is one of the greatest experiments in physics. Initially it was performed to prove the wave nature of light. Later on, it was also performed on electrons to prove its wave nature. But the light quanta i.e. photons or the electrons passing through a 'double slit' will exhibit interference only when we don't try to know which slit the particle is using while passing through. Any of our 'acts of knowing' disturbs the system and its coherence. This results in the disappearance of the interference pattern. The message is, don't disturb creative persons. They are sensitive. Let them remain in their world and allow them to finish their job. If we disturb and hurt them during the process of creation, they may stop creating.

Creators and Communicators both have their roles

There are two categories of particles. The fermions (electrons and protons like particles) are the particles which create matter. They follow Pauli's exclusion principle. According to this principle, not more than one particle can be accommodated in a single state. This gives us again a message, don't disturb creative people and let them remain alone as other's presence distracts them and affects their creativity. Like fermions, the creator of matter, we have bosons too. Contrary to fermions, they have no restriction on their entry in any state. Bosons interact with matter and provide a communication channel. They give us information about the existence of matter. Without bosons (photons like particles), we would have not known about the matter i.e. about the creation. In society both creators and communicators are important and are essential. Physics guides us to help creators and communicators for healthy growth of society.

Partiality is inherent

In case of β-decay, physicist Chien-Shiung Wu obtained an interesting result. When she placed a β-emitting source in a current carrying solenoid at very low temperature, she observed that the β-emission was maximum from that end which was south pole contrary to what was expected on the basis of symmetry. The Nature had this inherent partiality and Wu was able to discover it during weak interactions. This can be used to explain the meaning of left and right to extra-terrestrial intelligence, which otherwise would have not been possible. So, this partiality of Nature appears quite necessary but it is to help in making meaningful communication. Thus, the Nature has a soft corner towards its own creation. So, physics gives a message, one may become partial under some very special rare circumstances but it should not be to the extent of eating others opportunity. It should be to help and guide community.

Law of Nature - Interdependence and not the independence

One exists in relation to others. So, interdependence i.e. coexistence and not the solitariness is the law of Nature. Planetary system is a good example of coexistence and interdependence that gives a message to live in harmony. A slight change in environmental conditions may produce enormous changes. 'Butterfly effect' at one place may give birth to a storm thousands of kilometers away. So don't ignore any thing and relationship. One should always remember that even a small thing at times may become very important. So, the message that we get from physics is that nobody can survive ignoring others. Everybody is continuously interacting with his surroundings knowingly or unknowingly.

Time and locations are always important

We are familiar with coulombian repulsive interaction between protons. But when the protons are confined in a nucleus, they start attracting each other. A behavioural change appears as per the demand of the situation. The nuclear fusion is another example. The message for us is to remember that nothing is permanent. If it comes to survival, then one forgets the rivalry. So, don't get biased. Nobody's characteristics can be known with cent percent precision. It's the environment and the local conditions that decide the behaviour and characteristics observed during those moments. A person may behave and respond differently under police custody and before the court.

For survival, understanding is must

Two protons repel each other but when they are confined in a nuclear dimension, they forget their rivalry and come closer to attract each other. By remaining in the nucleus, they survive creatively to give rise 92 natural elements. We are the only living planet in our solar system and in the space we have explored so for. So like protons in the nucleus of an atom, we should also forget our differences and sign MoU (memorandum of understanding) to get involved in creativity.

Unity of creations

One comes across vast variety of complexities while observing physical phenomena. But man, through his natural instinct of searching the symmetries, has always made the things simpler. That's why; symmetry plays a vital role in understanding Nature through physics. One finds a common origin of all he observes in his surroundings. This led to unify mechanics and heat as thermodynamics. Similarly, the electricity, magnetism and optics got unified as electromagnetism. Then we came across short-range type of strong and weak interactions existing within nuclear region. The weak and electromagnetic interactions got unified and found to have common origin in the form of 'electro-weak interaction'. The 'electro-weak interaction' combined with the nuclear interaction and we developed standard model for understanding matter. The only problem that has remained to complete the scheme is to include the gravitational interaction. The physicists expect to achieve this unification too very soon.

The message from physics is that all entities of Nature, be it a tree, a mountain or a piece of gold, have common origin. There is an inherent unity behind all apparently different looking creations. A spherical ball is perfectly symmetric but when it is marked with a dot, it becomes asymmetric. We are to learn to see the ball without dot.

Possess, arrange and connect

In the electronic circuit, electronic components are arranged in proper way. If not, the circuit will not work.

So, possessing things is necessary but not sufficient. We need to know the order in which they are to be arranged. Further, it is not even sufficient to put them in order, one needs to learn connecting them properly.

The emerging world view from physics

The world-view has changed after the discoveries made in physics in the twentieth century. Three new kinds of physics emerged in this century. 'Relativity Physics' showed relative nature of matter, 'Quantum Physics' that told that there exists no objective reality and the 'Particle Physics' gave the message that all are deeply and inherently interconnected. So, when we talk of matter, we can't talk in isolation. Energy, space and time – all are intimately and inherently connected with matter. The connections are clearly visible in micro-world. In the twentieth century, physicists started looking seriously at the properties of matter. Thus, the physics of 20th century is entirely different than that of the 19th century. It showed that organic and ecological thinking is essential for the very existence. Holistic/Systemic approach is required to comprehend the universe. It further suggests us about the need of changing the mindset of the 19th century.

Need to change: Call from physics

From the history, we learn that many physicists got impressed by philosophers and started looking at Nature with positivism. The physics started developing logically and objectively. The major part of the physical progress that we see in our surroundings is the result of the development of physics up to the nineteenth century, so called 'classical physics'. A paradigm shift in the very foundation occurred when physicists started looking at the micro-world. Developments of the twentieth century physics not only took us in 'high-tech age' but also made us curious to find the connections with the spiritual world. The works of F. Capra, Gary Zukav, Fred Alan Wolf, Amit Goswami and David Bohm are worth mentioning. The new physics comprising of relativity physics, quantum physics and particle physics, suggest us to change our world-view from that of the 'reductionist' to the 'holistic'. It is interesting to learn about the way physicists could reach at these conclusions from simple clues they had collected from the physical world.

We are living in the 21st century and using 20th century technology but with an old mindset of the 19th century. This mindset has its roots in the scientific philosophy of Galileo, Descartes and Newton, where the systems were viewed as made of parts and were believed to work independent of each other. The world was viewed as machine and everything proceeded in certain and deterministic manner. This reductionist approach occupied the very heart of scientific working and did deeply influence the society. People's mindset got transformed. Even the body became machine for them. The science progressed and world got benefited a lot but soon the society started witnessing certain crises that resulted into severe problems like rising pollution, metabolic disturbances, appearance of some new kind of dreadful diseases and increased crimes. All these are different facets of the same problem, having a common origin in the reductionist approach resulting in fragmented worldview.

The 20th century brought great many changes in the 19th century's foundation of physics. The new physics gave rise birth to many technological revolutions that changed the world surrounding us. The new physics clearly indicated the existence of holistic view as against the 19th century fragmented worldview. It provided relativistic, organic, ecological, spiritual and holistic worldview, where interdependence and cooperation play dominant role.

Thus, the 20th century physics has shown us the way not only to create technological world of our choice but also to live therein by bringing necessary changes in mindset and rendering importance to all. In short, today's problems are related with the faulty mindset. A paradigm shift in the mindset is, thus, necessary in accordance with the findings of new physics. Without this, we will not be able to solve the problems and save the green earth.

Physics provides a platform where one can experience all that the human psyche is capable of. The knowledge of physics helps a lot as it induces rational thinking, youthful enthusiasm, self-control, inexhaustible curiosity, self-discipline and boldness. These are the basic elements required to face any challenge in life. In the next chapter, we will see some motivational quotes and tips.

9

MOTIVATIONAL QUOTES AND TIPS

Today, we live in information age. Any important thing happening in any remote corner of the world takes no time in becoming global. The information and communication network is expanding at tremendous pace today. Face book, LinkedIn, twitter etc. are there to connect, to comment, to get opinion and to find supporters. For those, who have interest and love for science, these platforms are of much value.

There are many researches in the field of physics that make catchy headlines in the media. These include any revolutionary idea, comprehensive theory, conceptual model, logical prediction, new observation etc. cosmic neutrinos, top quark, tau lepton, W and Z bosons, pulsar, black holes, cosmic x-ray sources, supernovae, cosmic microwave background radiation, superconductors, neutrino observatories, Big Bang-II, strongest thinnest material *graphene*, emerging field of *nano*-electronics '*spintronics*', quantum computers, Bose Einstein Condensate (BEC) etc. are amongst some of the media's headlines of the past few years. The 'God particle' (Higgs Boson) is the latest one.

Looking back, we recall the feelings expressed by Edwin Powell Hubble through the words 'Equipped with his five senses, man explores the universe around him and calls the adventure Science'. Truly, science, specially, physics is adventurous. It is a pleasure giving human creative activity like art, music or photography. But it requires a different approach. It gives pleasure when we learn to observe and think differently. Physics will emerge even if we are not aiming at. David Bohm pointed out the importance in the quote 'The ability to perceive or think differently is more important than the knowledge gained'. Ervin Schrödinger's words 'The task is ... not so much to see what no one has yet seen; but to think what nobody has yet thought, about that which everybody sees' also guide us.

Curiosity about anything that interests us is important. Richard P. Feynman's words 'You can know the name of a bird in all the languages of the world, but when you're finished, you'll know absolutely nothing whatever about the bird... So let's look at the bird and see what it's doing -- that's what counts.'

Any location that makes us curious becomes a point of self-enquiry. Any query or minute observation that we take becomes a seed of thought. When these seeds are sown in the fertile soil of mind, watered by 'imagination' and 'logics', we get the fruits of physics.

Physics 'flows' in the stream of logic. Any point may be the starting point. 'Think of colour, pitch, loudness, heaviness and hotness. Each is the topic of a branch of physics' as once quoted by Benoit Mandelbrot. Moving with the flow makes our journey effortless. In case of difficulties and hurdles, accessible help-lines are there. Inspiration is also needed while learning physics. We need to create our own sources of inspiration to remain self-motivated. As mentioned earlier, for this we may read life-history of scientists who worked under very odd circumstances. We need not worry. We should forget the unhappy experiences of the past, if any. Everything is understandable. But most of us don't agree with this. That's why, Einstein made the statement that 'the most incomprehensible thing about the world is that it is comprehensible.' He added further that 'the eternal mystery of the world is its comprehensibility'. So, we should proceed to learn physics confidently and fearlessly.

There are some tips that help us while learning physics.

- ❖ We should always remember that we have enormous potential. Remember the words of Marie Curie that 'Life is not easy for any of us. But what of that? We must have perseverance and above all confidence in ourselves. We must believe that we are gifted for something and that this thing must be attained'. So, the attitude of our mind should be such that it does not give up too easily. It is necessary at the beginning when the chances of losing heart, concentration and confidence are enormous.

- ❖ We should be watchful, thoughtful, confident and careful. We should not be afraid of going deeper in the subject. Remember what Marie Curie has guided through her quotation 'Nothing in life is to be feared, it is only to be understood. Now is the time to understand more, so that we may fear less'.

- Don't pay attention on what others are saying. Remember the words of Galileo Galilei that 'In questions of science, the authority of a thousand is not worth the humble reasoning of a single individual'. So, we should never lose faith in our logic and reasoning.

- We should not be biased. Albert Einstein's suggestion that 'a man should look for what is, and not for what he thinks should be'.

- We should find some moments to be relaxed. Actually, the ideas come during those moments. Paul A. M. Dirac shared his experience on how he used to get ideas. 'I found the best ideas usually come, not when one was actively striving for them, but when one was in a more relaxed state... I used to take long solitary walks on Sundays, during which I tended to review the current situation in a leisurely way. Such occasions often proved fruitful, even though (or perhaps because) the primary purpose of the walk was relaxation and not research. The words of Heisenberg are also worth recalling in this context. He has written about his experience in following words: 'it was about three o'clock at night when the final result of the calculation (which gave birth to quantum mechanics) lay before me ... At first I was deeply shaken ... I was so excited that I could not think of sleep. So I left the house ... and awaited the sunrise on top of a rock'.

- When we do something, mistakes are inevitable. But learning from mistakes is that what is required. Humphrey Davy shared his experiences through these words 'I have learned more from my mistakes than from my successes'.

- We should look around again and again but with different thinking. Michael Faraday's words 'Water is to me, I confess, a phenomenon which continually awakens new feelings of wonder as often as I view it.' So, its new thinking and new vision, that is important to have new feelings and new ideas.

- Arthur Eddington once said 'we often think that when we have completed our study of one, we know all about two, because 'two' is 'one and one.' We forget that we still have to make a study of 'and'. This is very inspiring for us when we have a feeling of complacency. It is the 'and' that always survives and invites us.

- Have child-like curiosity. Raise doubts and put questions. Curie enjoyed and got new insights. Listen what she says in her quote 'all my life through, the new sights of Nature made me rejoice like a child'. It is the child living in us that is important.

- When curiosity takes birth. Few questions appear before us. The answers depend on the type and quality of the question. It is the way of questioning that is important. Heisenberg once told, 'What we observe is not Nature itself but Nature exposed to our method of questioning. Our scientific work in physics consists in asking questions about Nature in the language that we possess and in trying to get an answer from the experiment by the means that are at our disposal'.

- When we meet a paradox, remember Neils Bohr's words 'How wonderful that we have met this paradox. Now we have some hope of making progress. Discover a physicist living in us by learning how to observe and listen. We will definitely get new light, new vision.

- When we reach at conflicting results, we should not ignore them. Believing this to be a deeper truth, we should try to find the hidden meaning. Neils Bohr reminds us about the old saying of the two kinds of truth. 'To the one kind belongs statements so simple and clear that the opposite assertion obviously could not be defended. The other kind, the so-called 'deep truths', is statements in which the opposite also contains deep truth'.

- We are living in the knowledge century. Recall Benjamin Franklin's words that "an investment in knowledge pays the best interest.'

- If we think we can, we can. If we think we can't, we can't. Our thinking decides whether to move or not. So, we should not sit quiet, because of our negative thinking. 'Nothing happens until something moves'. 'Look deep in Nature, and then you will understand everything better' as quoted by Einstein. So, move around and discover physics.

These are some of the tips. But this is not the end. We may also add few more guiding tips based on our experiences. With these, let us have the courage to be impatient and enter into the world of physics. Our journey is going to be adventurous because the paths may not be smooth and straight. We may find ups and downs, turns and twists. But we will certainly get thrilling experience of roller coasters and rides. Welcome…!!

References

L. Tarasov, This Amazingly Symmetrical World, Mir, 1986

10 Beautiful Examples of Symmetry in Nature, http://listverse.com/2013/04/21/10-beautiful-examples-of-symmetryin-nature/

Anu and Parmanu - Indian ideas about Atomic physics by Lobsan Payat
http://www.newsfinder.org/site/more/anu_and_parmanu_indian_ideas_about_atomic_physics/

Science in Ancient Greece http://www.crystalinks.com/greekscience.html Inventions and Discoveries of Ancient Greek Scientists
http://ancienthistory.about.com/od/sciencemedicine/tp/042810GreekScientificInventions.htm

History of Science and Technology in the Indian Subcontinent, http://en.wikipedia.org/wiki/History_of_science_and_technology_in_the_Indian_subcontinent

Ideas and Opinions by Albert Einstein, Rupa& Co., 2006

Hanbury Brown, The Wisdom of Science, Cambridge University Press, 1986

Peter Atkins, Creation Revisited, Penguin Books, 1992

Mani Bhaumik, The Cosmic Detective, Puffin Books, 2008

G. Venkararaman, Journey into Light – Life and Science of C.V. Raman, Penguin Books, 1994

The History of Clocks – 1, http://www.technologystudent.com/prddes1/hisclk1.html

K. M. Jain, Time-measuring Technique: Down up to femtosecond, Bull. I.A.P.T, Vol 18(7) July 2001. p-197.

Things Invented or Discovered by Accident http://science.howstuffworks.com/innovation/scientific-experiments/9things-invented-or-discovered-by-accident.htm#page=1

Ritter discovered ultraviolet light, http://coolcosmos.ipac.caltech.edu/cosmic_classroom/classroom_activities/ritter_bio.html

Herschel discovers infrared light, http://coolcosmos.ipac.caltech.edu/cosmic_classroom/classroom_activities/herschel_bio.html

The beginning of the Scientific Revolution, http://vlib.iue.it/carrie/texts/carrie_books/gilbert/23.html

Andrew Robinson, Einstein –A Hundred Years of Relativity, Oliver Craske, 2005

The discovery of electron spin, http://www.lorentz.leidenuniv.nl/history/spin/goudsmit.html

The discovery of positron, http://www.hep.man.ac.uk/babarph/babarphysics/positron.html

Hideki Yukawa, http://science.howstuffworks.com/dictionary/famous-scientists/physicists/hideki-yukawa-info.htm

Carl Anderson, http://www.aps.org/programs/outreach/history/historicsites/anderson.cfm

George Rochester, http://physicsworld.com/cws/article/news/2002/jan/10/george-rochester

Murray Gell-Mann, http://www.webofstories.com/play/murray.gellmann/76;jsessionid=C46F835010FFA4AB5FCF52DC7C831957

Discovering particles – Fundamental building blocks of the universe, http://www.ep.ph.bham.ac.uk/DiscoveringParticles/blocks/blocks/

Unprecedented neutrino discovery is a "Nobel Prize in the making",
http://io9.com/unprecedented-neutrino-discovery-is-a-nobel-prize-in-t-1469710608

K. M. Jain, Understanding Matter: Quark-lepton Model - Success and the Problems Ahead, Physics Education, October-December, 2002.P.193

George Gamow and J.A. Cleveland, Physics – Foundations and Frontiers, Prentice-Hall of India, 1963

N. Mukunda, Images of Twentieth Century Physics, Universities Press, 2000

ie-Physics, Experiment VI-5, Artificial Decay, http://d1068036.site.myhosting.com/ePhysics.f/labVI_5.html

AjoyGhatak, Special Theory of Relativity, Viva Books, 2009

Stephen Hawking, The Theory of Everything, JaicoPublishng House, 2010

Stephen Hawking, The Grand Design, Bantam Press, 2010

John Boslough, Stephen Hawking's Universe, Avon Books, 1989

John North, Astronomy and Cosmology, Fontana Press, 1994

Arthur I. Miller, Early Quantum Electrodynamics, Cambridge University Press, 1994

Joseph Silk, On the shores of the unknown: a short history of the universe, Cambridge University Press, (2005)

Introduction to the constants for nonexperts, http://www.physics.nist.gov/cuu/Constants/introduction.html

Current advances: The fine-structure constant and quantum Hall effect http://www.physics.nist.gov/cuu/Constants/alpha.html

Richard P. Feynman, Six Not-So-Easy, Penguin Books, 1997

John Gribbin, In Search of Multiverse, Allen Lane, 2009

Dark Matter Sheds New Light on Our Understanding of Starburst Galaxies, http://www.cosmotography.com/images/starburst_galaxies.html

Gribbin, J. R.; Gribbin, M., Stardust: Supernovae and Life – The Cosmic Connection. Yale University Press, 2000

Fritz Albert Popp *et.el.* (Eds.), Electromagnetic Bio-Information, Urban & Schwarzenberg, 1989

Peter P. Gariaev, Boris I. Birshtein, Alexander M. Iarochenko, Peter J. Marcer, George G. Tertishny, Katherine A. Leonova, Uwekaempf, "The DNA-wave Biocomputer" at http://www.rialian.com/rnboyd/dna-wave.doc Science, 266, 11th November, 1994 pp. 1021-1024.

Maslow M.U., Gariaev P.P., Fractal Presentation of Natural Language Texts Genetic Code, 2nd International Conference on Quantitative Linguistics", QUALICO '94, Moscow, September 2024, 193-194, 1994.

Peter Tompkins and Christopher Bird, The Secret Life of Plants, HarperCollins, 2000

Fritzjof Capra, The Tao of Physics, Flamingo, 1982

Amit Goswami, God is Not Dead, Jaico Publishing House, 2009

Fritzjof Capra, The Turning Point, Flamingo, 1983

Fred Alan Wolf, Mind into Matter, Master Mind Books, 2002

Kit Pedler, Mind Over Matter – A scientific View of the Paranormal, Panther, 1981

Lynne McTaggart, The Field: The Quest for the Secret Force of the Universe, HarperCollins Publishers, 2003

K. M. Jain, Effects of potentization. British Homeopathic Journal 89, 155-156 (2000)

K. M. Jain, Paranormal in the eyes of Physicists, Experience, Vol. 4(3), March. 2000. p-27

ParamahansaYogananda, 'Autobiography of a Yogi', Jaico Publishing House, Bombay, 1975

Michio Kaku, Physics of the Impossible, Penguin Books, 2009

K. M. Jain, Moments of discoveries are the real sources of inspiration. Bull. I.A.P.T., Vol. 16 (5) 1999, p-135.

K. M. Jain, Only creative ideas can bring recognition for you. Bull. I.A.P.T., Aug. 1998, p-235

K. M. Jain, A New generation of Philosophers, Experience, Vol. 4(1), Jan. 2000, p-23.

Joseph Von Fraunhofer, https://www.princeton.edu/~achaney/tmve/wiki100k/docs/Joseph_von_Fraunhofer.html

The Mule Driver Who Measured the Universe, http://oneminuteastronomer.com/1562/mule-driver-measureuniverse/

Meghnad Saha - A Pioneer in Astrophysics, http://www.vigyanprasar.gov.in/scientists/saha/sahanew.htm

http://www.academia.edu/6253454/Michael_Faraday_and_James_Clerk_Maxwell_Different_Men_of_Science

Robert L. Weber, Pioneers of Science – Nobel Prize Winners in Physics, Adam Hilger, 1988

G.P. Snow, The Physicists, Bellew & Hington Publishers Ltd.

S. Ananthanarayanan, From the World of Science, Puffin Books, 2004

All Nobel Prizes in Physics, http://www.nobelprize.org/nobel_prizes/physics/laureates/

The Frontiers of Physics and Their Roles in Society, http://iopscience.iop.org/1402-4896/19/3/001

Quotes About Inspiration, http://www.goodreads.com/quotes/tag/inspiration

Marie Curie Quotes, http://www.brainyquote.com/quotes/authors/m/marie_curie.html

Humphry Davy Quotes http://www.brainyquote.com/quotes/authors/h/humphry_davy.html

Scientist Quotes, http://www.brainyquote.com/quotes/type/type_scientist.html

Science Quotes by Werner Heisenberg http://todayinsci.com/H/Heisenberg_Werner/HeisenbergWernerQuotations.htm

Quotations by Albert Einstein http://www.quotationspage.com/quotes/Albert_Einstein/

Science quotes by P.A.M. Dirac http://todayinsci.com/D/Dirac_Paul/DiracPaul-Quotations.htm

Science quotes by E. Schrödinger http://todayinsci.com/S/Schrödinger_Erwin/ SchrödingerErwin-

Quotations.htm Galileo Galilei Quotes, http://www.brainyquote.com/quotes/authors/g/galileo_galilei.html

David Bohm Quotes, http://www.brainyquote.com/quotes/authors/d/david_bohm.html

Michael Faraday Quotes, http://www.brainyquote.com/quotes/authors/m/michael_faraday.html

Edwin Powell Hubble Quotes, http://www.brainyquote.com/quotes/authors/e/edwin_powell_hubble.html

Steven Weinberg Quotes, http://www.brainyquote.com/quotes/authors/s/steven_weinberg.html

10 of the Greatest Quotes by Famous and Awesome Scientists http://timehuman.blogspot.in/2010/05/greatestscientist-quotes.html

Quotes About Physics, http://www.goodreads.com/quotes/tag/physics

Richard P. Feynman Quotes, http://www.goodreads.com/author/quotes/1429989.Richard_P_Feynman

The Qualities of Isaac Newton, http://www.mindmapinspiration.com/the-qualities-of-isaac-newton/

Bill Bryson, A short History of Nearly Everything, A Black Swan Book, 2003

A Brief (Incomplete) History of Light and Spectra, http://www.chemteam.info/Electrons/Spectrum-History.html

A History of Astrophysics and Cosmology, http://gatesofvienna.net/2003/11/a-history-of-astrophysics-andcosmology-2/

John Gribbin, Get Grip on New Physics, Weidenfeld and Nicolson, 1999

Tom Duncan Advanced Physics, John Murray (Publishers) Ltd., 1994

I.R. Kenyon, Superstrings, Oxford University Press, NY, 1997

James William Rohlf, Modern Physics (From α to z^0), John Wiley & Sons, 1994

John Gribbin, Q for Quantum, Weidenfeld & Nicolson, 1998

John Gribbin and Martin Rees, The Stuff of the Universe, Penguin Books, 1995

Rom Harre', Great Scientific Experiments, Phaidon, Oxford, 1981

Paul Davies, The New Physics, Cambridge, 1992

B.H. Bransden and C.J. Joachain, Introduction to Quantum Mechanics, Longman Scientific and Technical, 1989

Molecules at an Exhibition, John Emsley, Oxford University Press, 1998

J.J. Sakurai, Modern Quantum Mechanics, Addison-Wesley, 1999

David J. Griffiths, Introduction to Electromagnetism, Prentice Hall of India, 1995

G. Venkataraman, What Is Relaivity?, Universities Press (India) Limited, 1994

Y. Perelman, Physics Can Be Fun, Mir, 1986

Richard P. Feynmn, Surely You're Joking Mr. Feynman, Vintage, 1992